AF488025

Chateau d'Orquevaux

A TRAVELOGUE

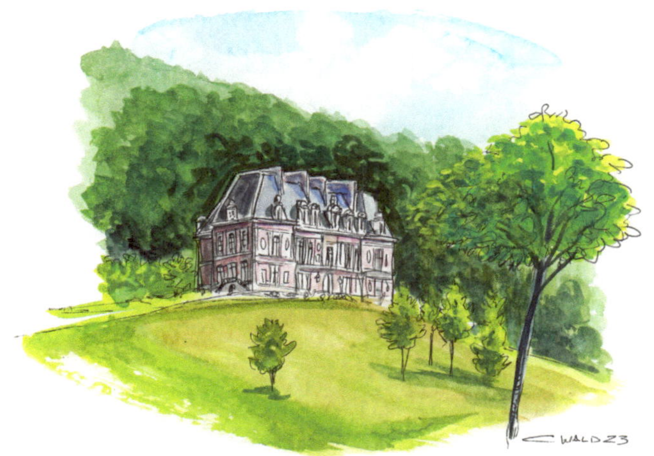

CHRISTINA WALD

'WHETHER YOU SUCCEED OR NOT IS IRRELEVANT.
THERE IS NO SUCH THING. MAKING YOUR UNKNOWN
KNOWN IS THE IMPORTANT THING'
— GEORGIA O'KEEFFE

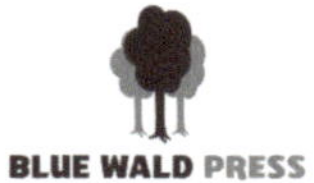

BLUE WALD PRESS

An Idea

EVERYTHING BEGINS WITH AN IDEA...

A thought appears out of the nothingness. A seed in the field of imagination... and then a flower...

Plucked out of the wilderness and manifested into reality.

I wonder how is that possible?

I can touch it now, so can you. All of it.

Land, sky and stone. It's here.

A manifestation of imagination. It's real. It's Art.
It's a work in progress with the unlimited potential to become a masterpiece for all to enjoy.

It was a dream, yes. But now so much more then that dream ever was...

It's only the beginning really...
Everything starts somewhere. And this starts here.

It's a beautiful thing...

Everything begins with an idea...

In my case, maybe the dream came first.

The sign outside the gate reads "Artists only".
Not really, of course. But the sign is there never the less.

There was a cry heard around the world. Outsiders welcome!
And you know who you are. We do too.

From the very start or pretty close to, we were just too many.
And we came from everywhere.

South Africa, Bulgaria, United States, Egypt, Nigeria, Israel, El Salvador and Australia, Saudi Arabia, China, Japan, India, The Netherlands, Mexico, Germany.
And the list goes on . . .

The residency had no history then. We're beginning to now.
I like the romance of thinking we are A band of bandits, lawless somehow.
But we aren't.

I like the idea of imagining we are a traveling circus, a carnival of sorts, with Jugglers, Fire breathers, and Sword Swallowers.
But we aren't.

Maybe there are elements of all of all that . . . but if true, then really for just brief moments.

We are all United by imagination and creativity and
As artists we are The Dreamers and The Idealists...

The simply creative types.
We are damaged and we are whole.
We are as we should be.

We are important and we are needed.
But so is everyone else.

No matter the story you choose to tell yourself.
All of You are important and all of you are needed.

Everything begins with an idea...

In my case, maybe the dream came first.

I really don't know anymore.

We have all set out on this journey and made our way here to this small village called Orquevaux, a Noah's ark of sorts.

We are the children of the universe.
We are Wives, mothers, and daughters.
We are Husbands, fathers and sons.
We are Addicts and loners. Introverts and Extroverts.
We are Musicians, poets and painters.
We are Writers, sculptors and filmmakers

We are the weirdos, philosophers and the so called losers...
Which we are not.

Outside the walls - labels and identities are rampant. But here,
The hope is, that they are not.

Here the hope is one of self discovery, exploration, and the tearing down of self imposed boundaries.

We are all here scratching the surface, and Searching for answers, in the hope, of finding a bit of truth and that which is real.

This is a special place...
And trying to capture it, while struggling to put it down in words, I feel adds little. This place speaks for itself. History is being written, and we are all a part of the story. Both the personal and the universal.

But Is it Art? Maybe.
Is it Bigger? Possibly.
Deeper? Definitely.

I believe that we are all in pursuit of that intangible something, and I believe that we are all trying to make it tangible...

That's what art is, Making the invisible visible.

Our job, our obligation even, is to make them see.

I will also tell you with complete certainty, that for those of us here who cultivate the land, oil the gears, and keep the lights on, that we take that same obligation seriously.

Everything begins with an idea.

In my case, maybe the dream came first.

- **Ziggy Attias**
Co-founder / Co-director, Chateau d' Orquevaux

Session One

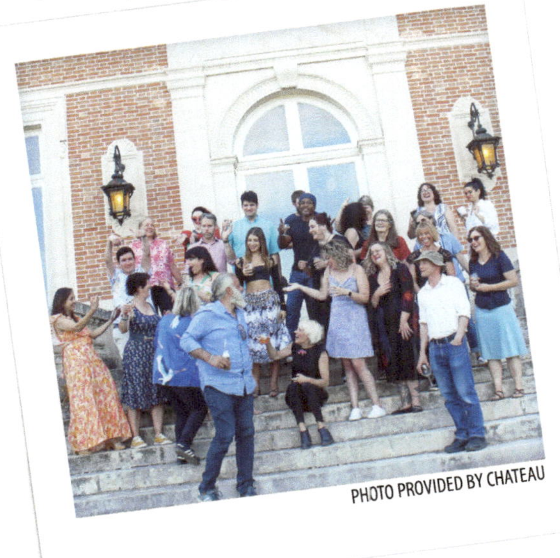

Pictured L to R: *Sonali, Mark, Roxy, Patricia, Shawna, Lori, Kat, Graham, Evan, Tatiana, Ziggy, Beulah, Chris, Christina, Maggie, Kayla, Ann, Lorine, Eleanor, Carina, Marie, Greg, Martha, Clair, Niki*

Session Two

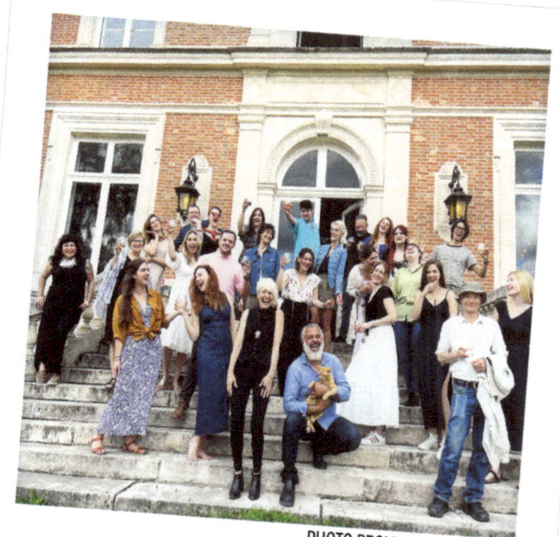

Pictured L to R: *Michelle, Jacqui, Laura, Victoria, Angus, Sonja, Brandon, Kat, Monica, Christina, Alison, Lauren, Beulah, Ziggy, Jennifer, Celine, Leah, Evan, Mike, Kristine, Libia, Erin, Rachel, Jonathan, Greg, Leigh*

Introduction

I SUBMITTED MY APPLICATION TO THE CHATEAU D'ORQUEVAUX RESIDENCY ON AUGUST 8TH, 2020.

IT HAD BEEN A ROUGH YEAR FOR EVERYONE ON THE PLANET. COVID CLOSED DOWN EVERYTHING SUDDENLY IN MARCH. I HAD TO CANCEL TRIPS TO BARCELONA, HONG KONG, AND IRELAND.

I HAD BEEN ON MANY ARTIST RETREATS AND SKETCH TRIPS AND ENJOYED THE ADVENTURES OF MEETING NEW CREATIVES IN BEAUTIFUL LANDSCAPES AROUND THE WORLD. I HAD BEEN TO YELLOWSTONE, NORTH CAROLINA, WASHINGTON, AND MY FRIEND AMY BOGARD'S SKETCH JOURNAL WORKSHOPS IN TAOS AND ANTIGUA ON OTHER ART ADVENTURES.

MY FIRST SELF-DESCRIBED 'RESIDENCY' WAS IN BERGEN, NORWAY, JUNE 2019 WITH LIGHT GREY ART LAB. IT WAS SO ENJOYABLE THAT I STARTED TO RESEARCH OTHER RESIDENCY OPTIONS. I SAW THE CHATEAU'S WEBSITE LISTED ON A RESIDENCY WEBSITE, BOOKMARKED IT, AND LET IT PERCOLATE IN THE BACK OF MY MIND.

I APPLIED IN AUGUST 2020 WITH A MIXTURE OF HOPE AND WISHFUL THINKING AND WAS ACCEPTED IN SEPTEMBER, THE DAY AFTER MY BIRTHDAY.

OF COURSE, WE WERE STILL IN COVID TIMES AND TRAVEL RESTRICTIONS WERE IN PLACE. IT WAS A LEISURELY WAIT UNTIL EVERYTHING ALIGNED. ONCE WE WERE PERMITTED TO TRAVEL AGAIN, JO ANN, MY FRIEND WHO WAS JOINING ME FOR THE FIRST TWO WEEKS, AND I HAD TO AGREE ON A TIME AND IT HAD TO BE AVAILABLE.

WE SETTLED ON JULY 2023.

SINCE I WAS GOING TO BE THERE FOR A MONTH, IT GAVE ME THE OPPORTUNITY TO CRAFT A TRAVELOGUE. I LOVE DOCUMENTING MY TRAVELS BUT TEND NOT TO WRITE ABOUT THEM. THIS WAS MY ATTEMPT TO CHANGE THAT AND KEEP A DAILY JOURNAL.

– CHRISTINA WALD 2023

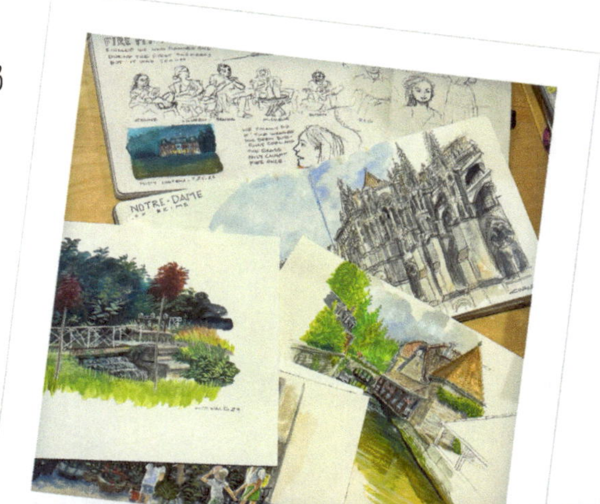

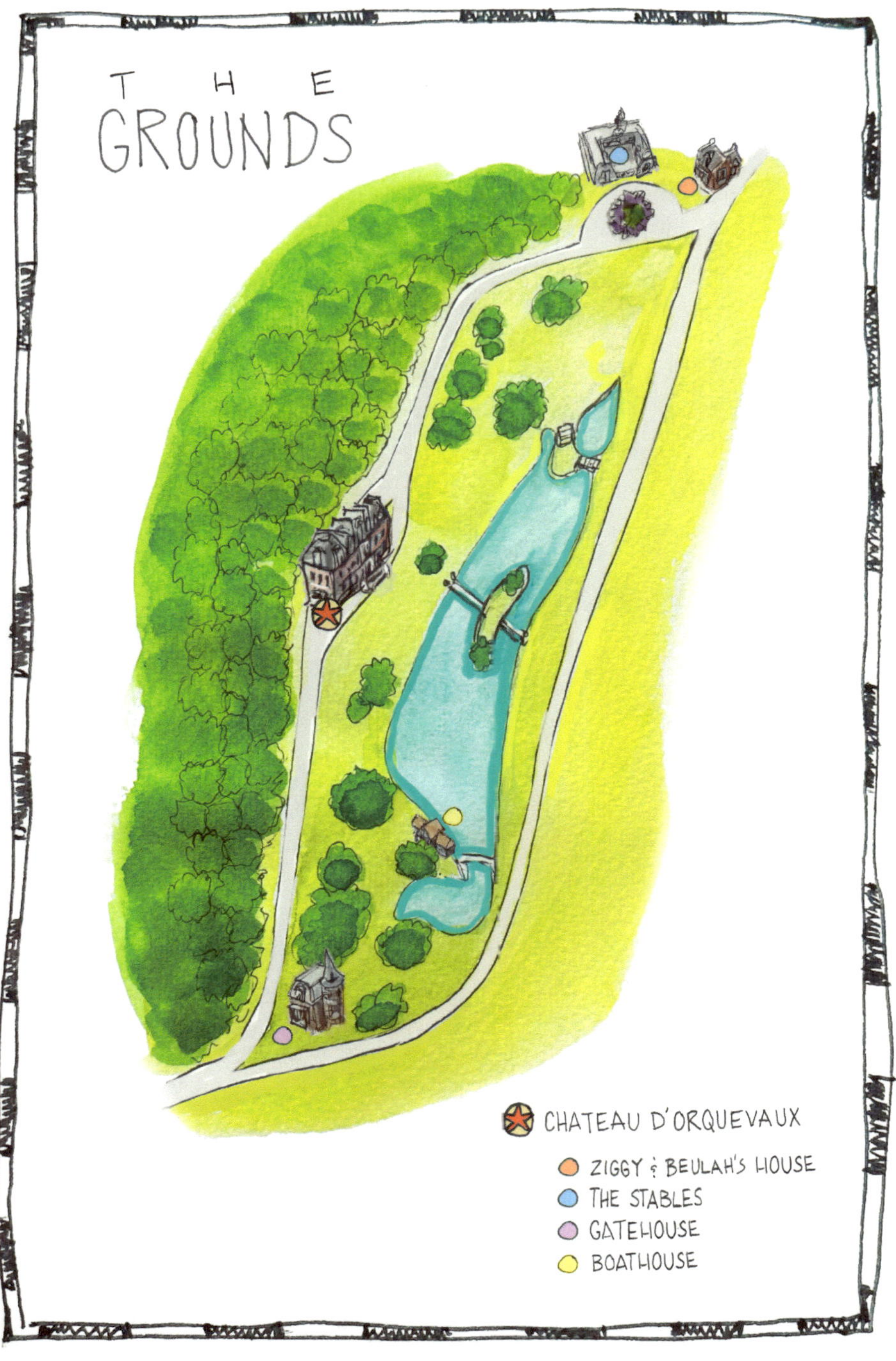

THE
GROUNDS
CHATEAU D'ORQUEVAUX
ZIGGY & BEULAH'S HOUSE
THE STABLES
GATEHOUSE
BOATHOUSE

Epic Clouds

HALF OF TRAVEL IS ANTICIPATION.

PLANNING FOR THIS RESIDENCY WAS IN SLOW MOTION FOR OVER A YEAR. MY FRIEND, JO ANN BERGER, APPLIED SOON AFTER I DID AND WE ASKED TO BE SCHEDULED AT THE SAME TIME EVEN THOUGH SHE WAS ONLY THERE FOR TWO WEEKS. WE NEGOTIATED AND EVENTUALLY SETTLED ON JULY WHICH WORKED FOR ALL OF OUR SCHEDULES.

WE BOOKED OUR FLIGHTS, RENTAL CAR, AND HOTEL IN PARIS FOR THE FIRST COUPLE OF DAYS. I WAS ALSO PREPARING FOR A TRIP TO AUCKLAND SO FRANCE WAS A LITTLE ON THE BACK-BURNER WHILE I HELPED MANAGE A HUGE SOCIAL MEDIA SPONSORSHIP CAMPAIGN WITH THE URBAN SKETCHERS SYMPOSIUM. MY FAMILY WAS ALSO ON THAT TRIP SO THERE WAS A LOT OF PLANNING INVOLVED. JO ANN PINGED ME EVERY COUPLE OF WEEKS TO NUDGE ME SO I HAD EVERYTHING BOOKED.

TRAVEL DAY.

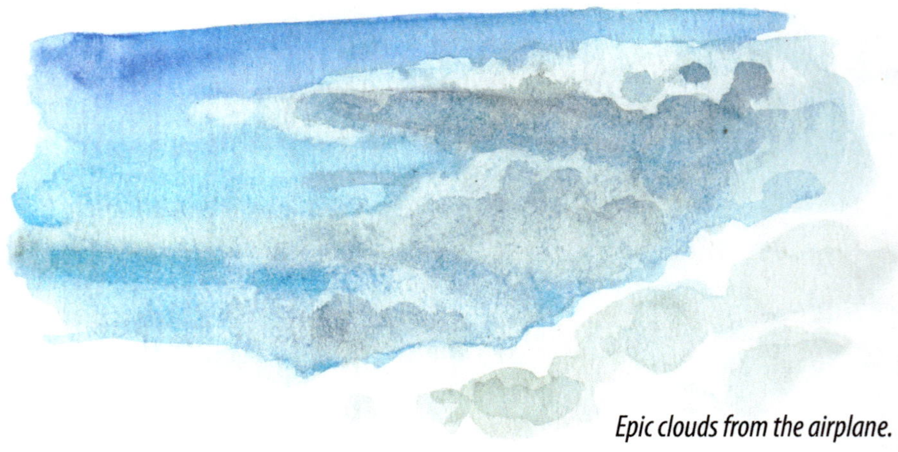

Epic clouds from the airplane.

JO ANN BOOKED HER DIRECT FLIGHT EARLY WHILE I SHOPPED AROUND. IN THE END, I BOOKED FROM CINCINNATI TO NICE, FRANCE VIA ATLANTA. IT SEEMED LIKE A GOOD IDEA AT THE TIME ANYWAY. I HAD HOPED TO MEET SOME FAMILY HEADED TO MARSEILLES WHICH COMPLETELY FAILED TO WORK OUT. I MADE AN EASYJET RESERVATION FOR NICE TO PARIS. THAT MADE THE ITINERARY MORE COMPLICATED THAN IT NEEDED TO BE. GOLDEN RULE OF TRAVEL: TIME IS MORE COSTLY THAN A FEW DOLLARS.

THE TIME BETWEEN RETURNING IN APRIL AND LEAVING JULY 1ST WAS A BLUR. I PRINTED AND FULFILLED MY BOOK KICKSTARTER, FINISHED BOOK ILLUSTRATIONS FOR A CHAPTER BOOK, SKETCHED ANOTHER, AND MENTORED AN AUTHOR I WORK WITH ON HER FIRST KICKSTARTER.

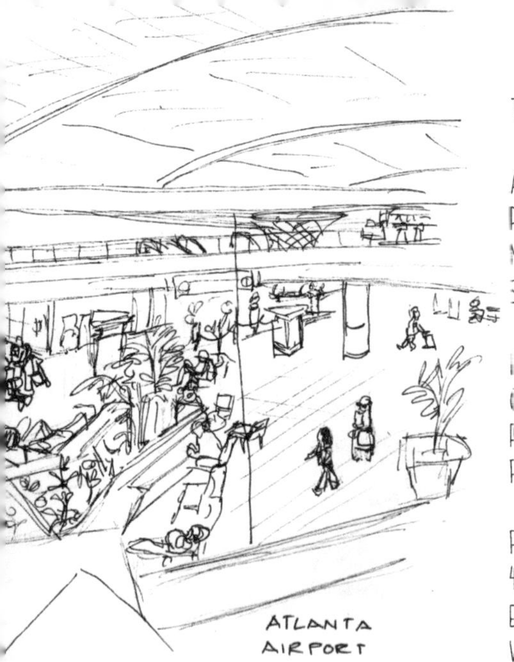

ATLANTA
AIRPORT

THE NEXT THING I KNEW. I WAS OFF TO THE AIRPORT.

AFTER AN INITIAL DELAY FROM CVG TO ATL. I HAD PLENTY OF TIME TO MAKE THE FLIGHT TO NICE. I SAT NEXT TO THE GATE TO PENSACOLA FOR A WHILE AND SKETCHED.

IT WAS A HOLIDAY WEEKEND AND THE FLIGHT WAS OVERBOOKED AND DELTA WAS TRYING TO FIND NINE PEOPLE WILLING TO TAKE A GIFT CARD TO TAKE A DIFFERENT FLIGHT THAT DID NOT LEAVE UNTIL TUESDAY!

FEW PEOPLE SEEMED TO WANT TO GIVE UP THEIR JULY 4TH TO STAY IN ATLANTA FOR A FEW DAYS. THEY EVENTUALLY OFFERED $1200 TO EACH PASSENGER WILLING TO FORFEIT THEIR TRIP.

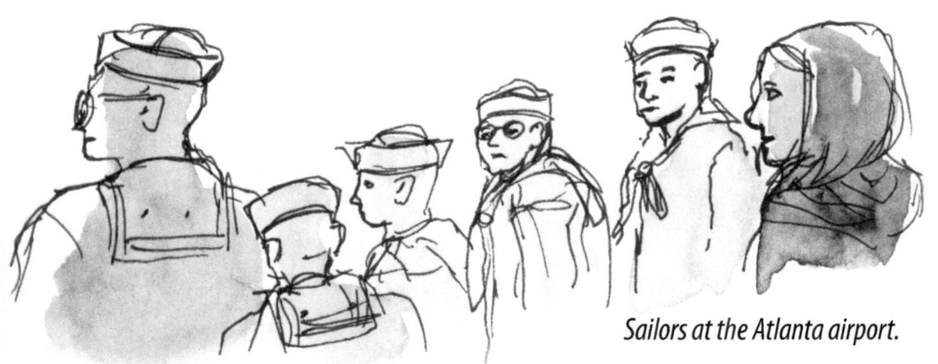

Sailors at the Atlanta airport.

THAT DID NOT SEEM LIKE ENOUGH TO ME.

I WAS VERY LATE GETTING INTO PARIS.

I HAD TO TAKE A 1 HOUR SHUTTLE RIDE FROM THE EASYJET AIRPORT OUTSIDE OF PARIS AND THEN A TAXI TO THE HOTEL. IT REMINDED ME THAT SIMPLE ITINERARIES ARE MORE EFFICIENT AND IN THE LONGTERM MORE INEXPENSIVE.

JO ANN SKETCHED AT A CUTE CAFE AND BEFRIENDED EVERYONE THERE UNTIL I ARRIVED AFTER 8 PM.

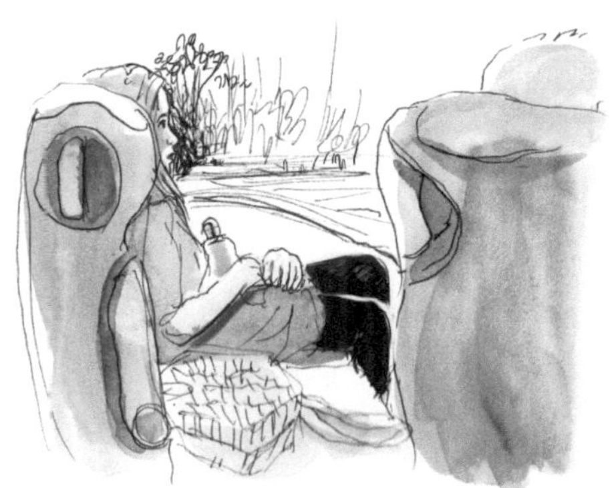

Bus from Beavais to Paris.

Paris

WE HAD A DAY IN PARIS! WE STARTED THE DAY IN A LEISURELY FASHION. MUSEUMS USUALLY REQUIRE TICKETS IN ADVANCE THESE DAYS SO WE SKETCHED AT A CRÊPERIE AND STROLLED THROUGH LUXEMBOURG GARDENS INSTEAD. A BAND FROM A SCHOOL IN SCOTLAND WAS PLAYING BAGPIPES AND INTERESTING ARRANGEMENTS OF POPULAR TUNES IN ONE OF THE MAIN GAZEBOS.

WE SKETCHED AT A FOUNTAIN WITH DUCKS AND A SCULPTURE OF CYCLOPS BEING JILTED BY THE GIRL HE WANTED.

WE FINISHED THE DAY AT LIZA. A LEBANESE RESTAURANT WHERE WE GOT A RIDICULOUS DINNER FOR TWO PEOPLE. IT CAME WITH FOUR DESSERTS!

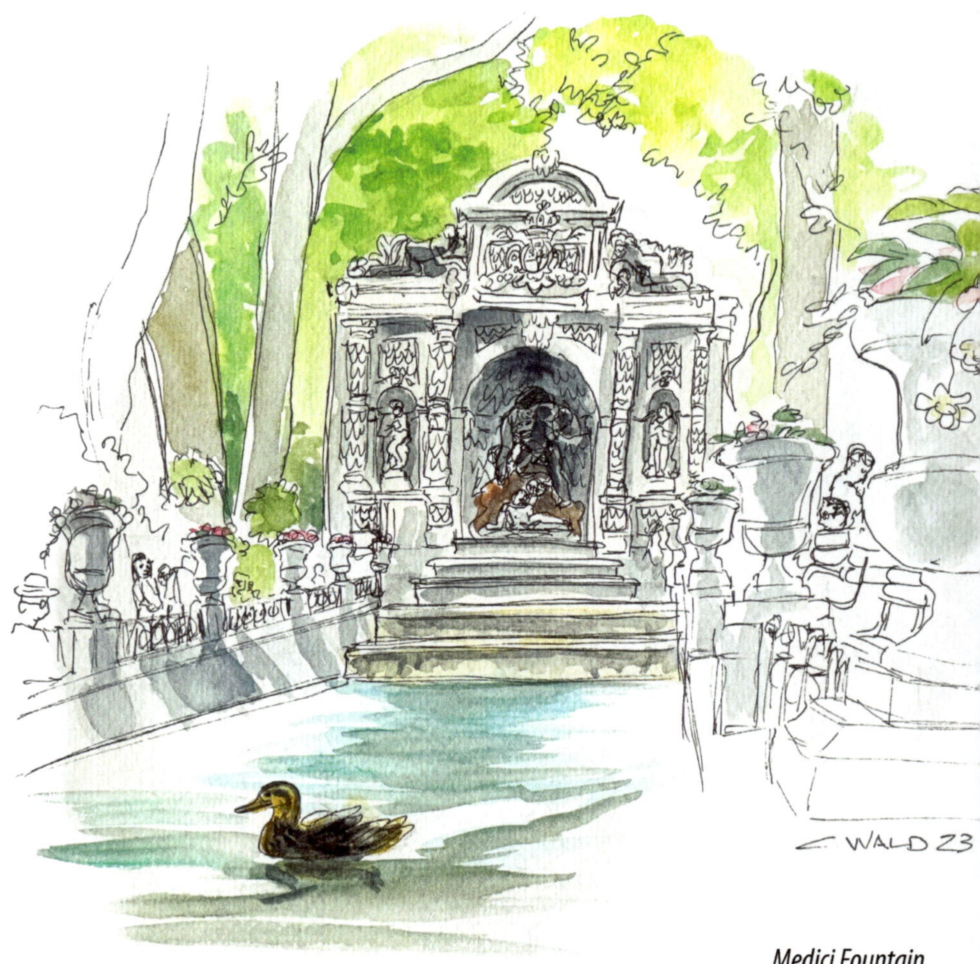

Medici Fountain.

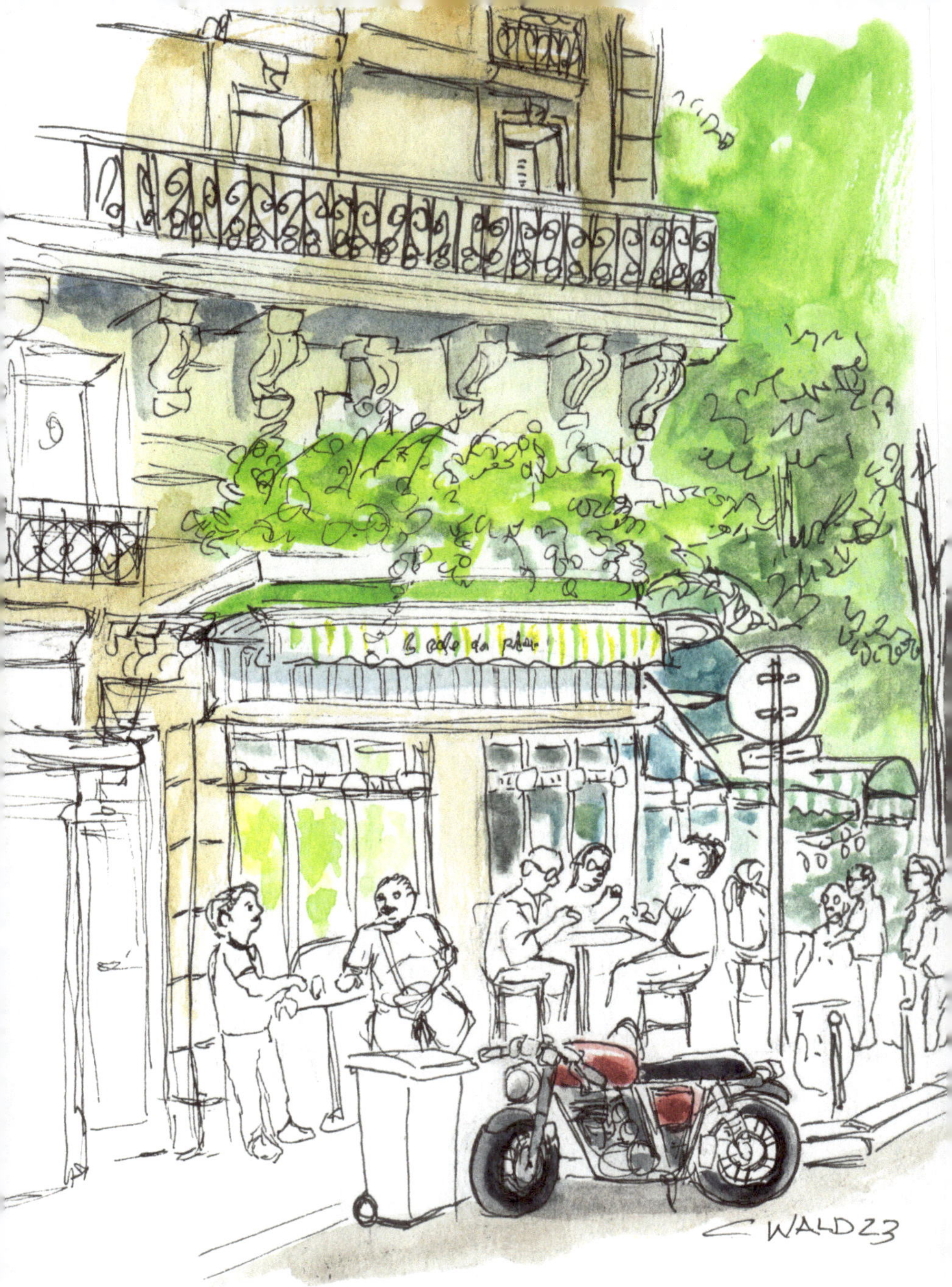

COEUR de BREIZH
authentique crêperie bretonne

Dinner at Liza

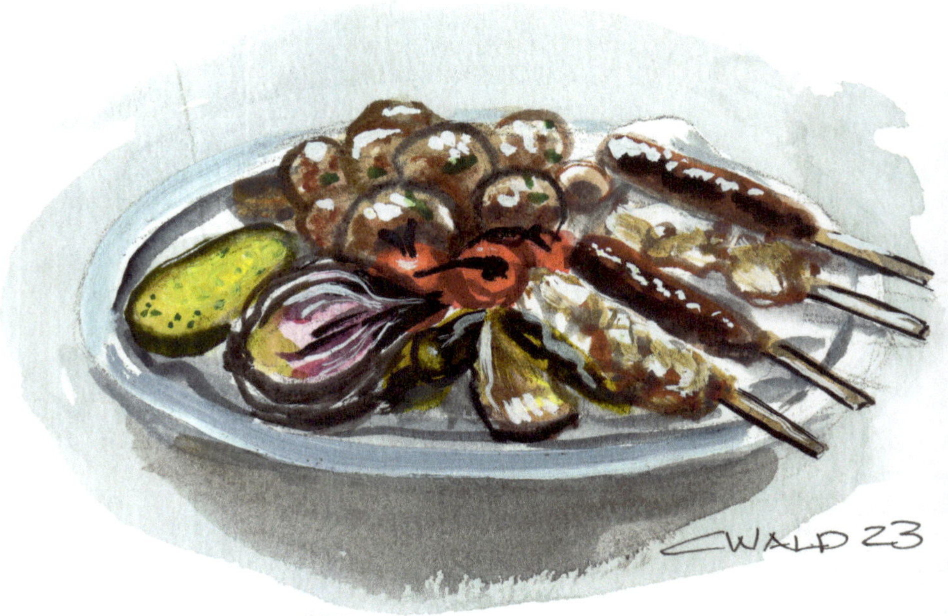

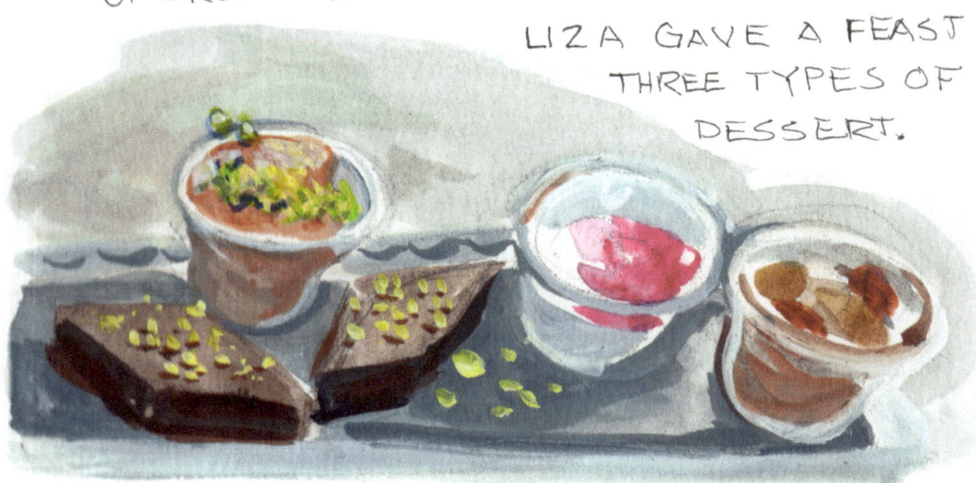

LIZA

FINAL DINNER IN PARIS AFTER A DAY
OF SKETCHING AT LUXEMBOURG GARDENS.

LIZA GAVE A FEAST
THREE TYPES OF
DESSERT.

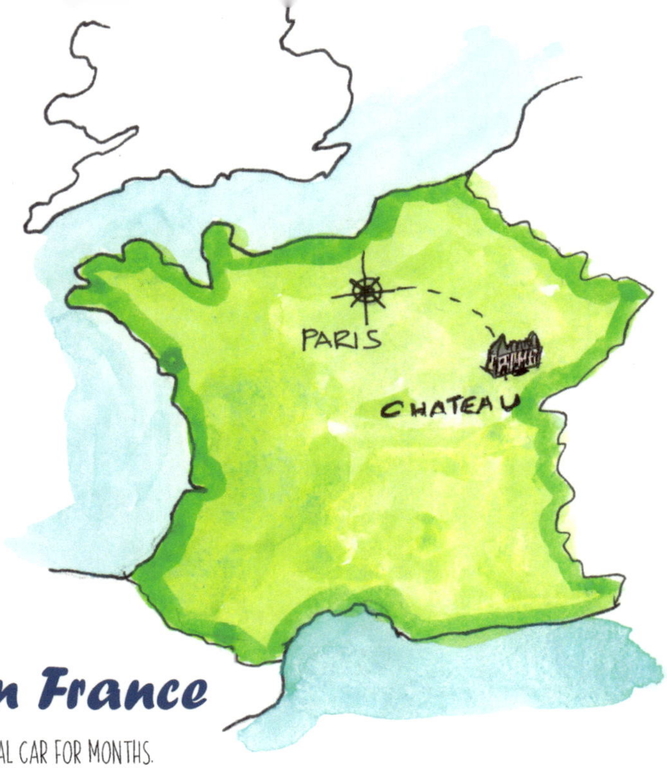

Driving in France

WE DISCUSSED GETTING A RENTAL CAR FOR MONTHS.

AT FIRST, THE PLAN WAS FOR ME TO LEARN TO DRIVE A STICK SHIFT SINCE AUTOMATIC TRANSMISSIONS ARE SUPPOSED TO BE MORES EXPENSIVE AND HARDER TO FIND. I HAD CAJOLED MY FRIEND KATIE TO TEACH ME HOW TO DRIVE ONE IN THE FEW MONTH BEFORE WE LEFT.

AFTER A FEW HOURS OF MAKING THE CAR, LURCH, SHUTTER, AND DIE OVER AND OVER. I REALIZED MY NON-STOP SCHED-ULE WOULDN'T ALLOW FOR MULTIPLE DRIVING LESSONS.

LUCKILY FRENCH LAW CAME TO THE RESCUE! APPARENTLY IN FRANCE, ALL LUGGAGE HAS TO BE IN THE TRUNK SO WE NEEDED A BIGGER CAR. ON THE COSTCO SITE WHERE WE WERE RENTING THE CAR, AUTOMATIC WAS THE ONLY CHOICE.

ALTHOUGH THE COST FOR THE BIGGER CAR WAS MORE THAN WE PLANNED, IT WAS WORTH IT IN THE END. ALTHOUGH WE WERE EXTREMELY CAREFUL. SO WE THOUGHT AT LEAST. WE HAD A COUPLE TRAFFIC TICKETS MAILED TO US WHEN WE GOT BACK HOME. THERE IS NOT GRACE FOR DRIVING ABOVE THE SPEED LIMIT.

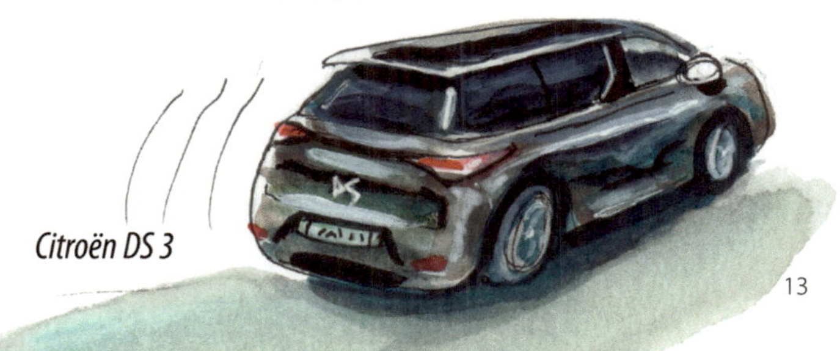

Citroën DS 3

Journey to Orquevaux

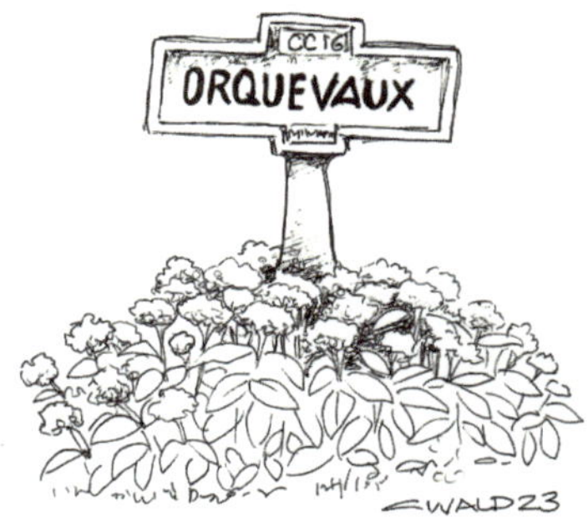

"A CREATIVE LIFE IS AN AMPLIFIED LIFE. IT'S A BIGGER LIFE, A HAPPIER LIFE, AN EXPANDED LIFE, AND A HELL OF A LOT MORE INTERESTING LIFE. LIVING IN THIS MANNER— CONTINUALLY AND STUBBORNLY BRINGING FORTH THE JEWELS THAT ARE HIDDEN WITHIN YOU— IS A FINE ART, IN AND OF ITSELF."

– ELIZABETH GILBERT

IT WAS AN UNEXPECTED HURDLE TRYING TO EXPLAIN TO OUR TAXI DRIVER THAT WE WERE GOING TO THE AIRPORT TO GET A CAR, NOT TO FLY A PLANE. FORTUNATELY, HE MADE AN EFFORT TO UNDERSTAND US.

THE DRIVE FROM THE AIRPORT TO THE CHATEAU WAS A BIT OVER THREE HOURS. JO ANN TOOK THE FIRST TURN DRIVING WHEN WE ENCOUNTERED OUR FIRST TOLL ROAD. SHE WAS SO FLUSTERED THAT SHE DID NOT TAKE THE TICKET THAT DETERMINES THE TOLL.

WHEN WE ARRIVED AT THE PAYMENT BOOTH, A KIND WOMAN LET US DETERMINE THE AMOUNT OWED FROM PARIS AND THE CRISIS WAS AVERTED.

THE DRIVE GOES FROM THE BUSTLING CITY TO RURAL EXTREME. THE LAST HOUR OF THE DRIVE WAS SUNFLOWER AND HAY FIELDS AND ALMOST NO CARS. IT WAS SO REMOTE. GOOGLE MAPS FINALLY INDICATED WE WERE CLOSE AND WE DROVE THROUGH POISSON AND EVENTUALLY INTO ORQUEVAUX.

THE FINAL, STEEP GRAVEL DRIVEWAY MADE ME EXTREMELY GRATEFUL WE HAD AN AUTOMATIC TRANSMISSION.

The Residency

DAY 1

WE WERE THE FIRST TO ARRIVE AND EVERYONE MET US AT THE CAR AND HELPED US UNLOAD. REMI AND CARINA SHOWED US TO OUR ROOMS AND STUDIOS.

WE ALSO HAD A BRIEF TOUR FOLLOWED BY CHAMPAGNE, SNACKS, AND INTRODUCTIONS. JO ANN DECIDED TO DON AN ALTER EGO AND INTRODUCE HERSELF AS ROXY.

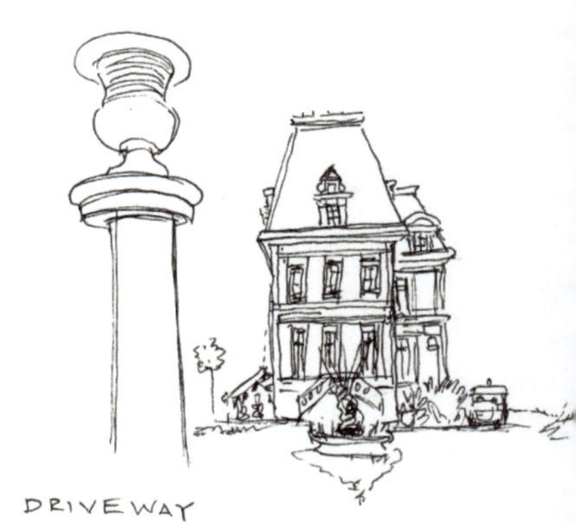

DRIVEWAY

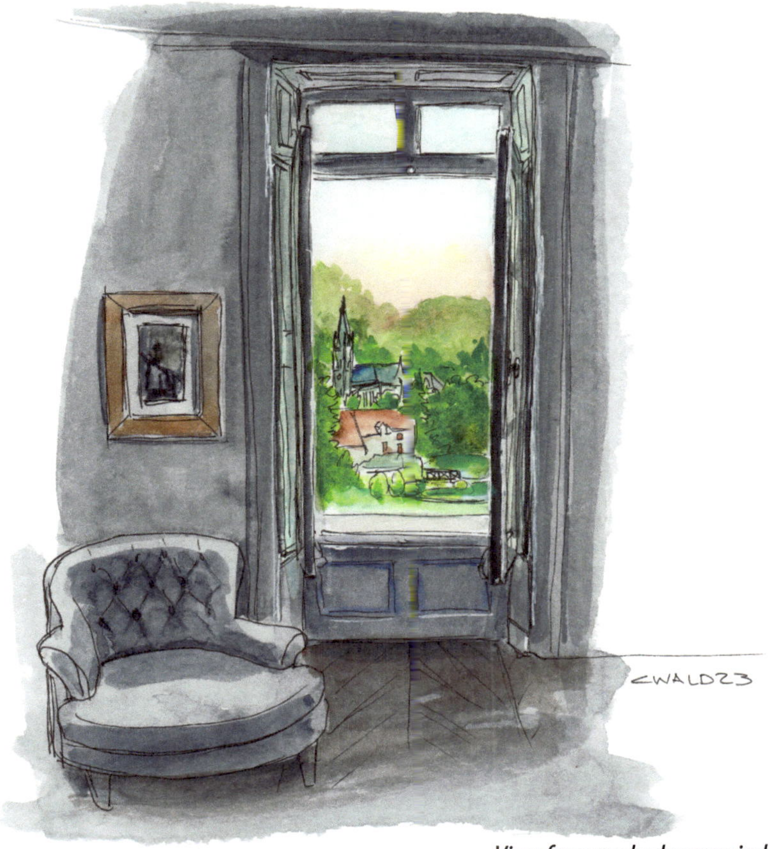

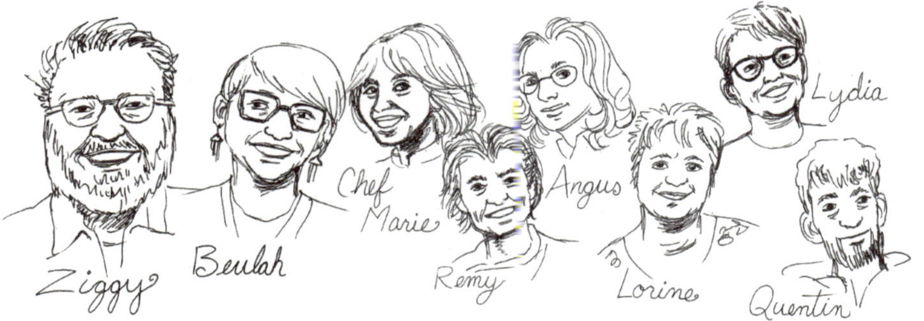

View from my bedroom window.

CO-FOUNDER AND CO-DIRECTORS, **ZIGGY** AND **BEULAH**, STRIVE TO PUT TOGETHER A DIVERSE AND INTERESTING GROUP OF ARTISTS IN EACH TWO WEEK SESSION. IT IS HARD TO BELIEVE THAT YOU WILL LEARN EVERYONE'S NAME. THEY ALSO HAVE A DEDICATED AND FRIENDLY STAFF. CHEF MARIE, QUENTIN, LYDIA, AND LORINE PREPARE ALL THE WONDERFUL MEALS SEVEN DAYS A WEEK AND REMY IS IN CHARGE OF THE GROUNDS. ANGUS, MARIE'S SON, HELPS OUT WITH THE RESIDENCY. THERE ARE MANY OTHERS THAT HELP OUT TOO WITH CLEANING AND RENOVATION. IT TAKES A LOT PEOPLE TO MANAGE A VENTURE LIKE THIS.

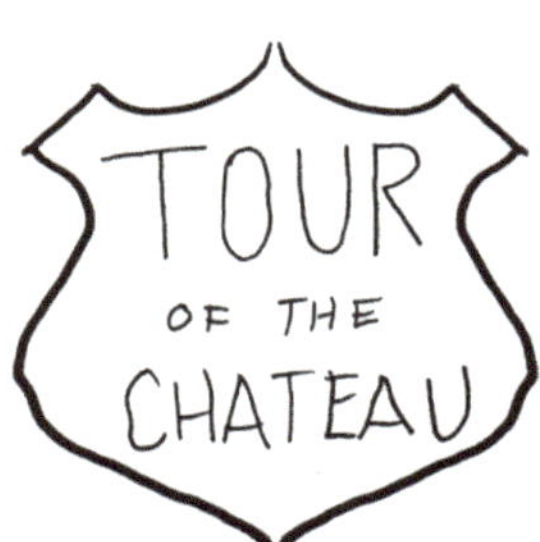

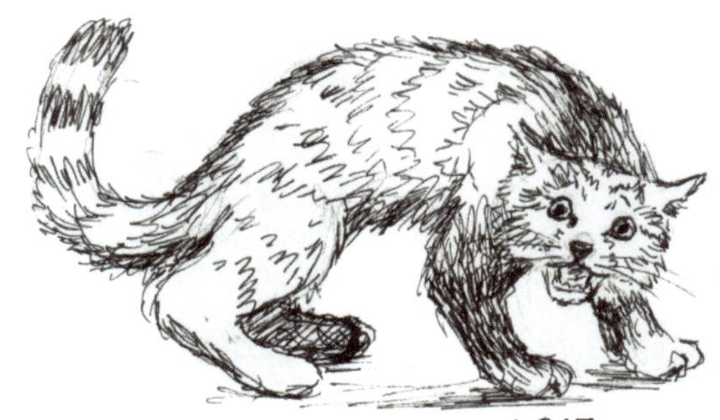
TAXIDERMY CAT

WE HAD OUR FIRST AND ABUNDANT WELCOME DINNER OF BOEUF BOURGUIGNON WHILE WE GOT ACQUAINTED WITH THIS GROUP OF CREATORS. ONLY FOUR OF US WERE THERE THE FULL MONTH AND WE FOUND EACH OTHER QUICKLY. IT IS SO HARD AT FIRST TO ASSESS WHO YOU WILL BE MOST COMPATIBLE WITH IN A NEW GROUP OF PEOPLE. I ALSO HAD COME BURDENED BY DEADLINES. I HAD A BOOK COVER DUE JULY 10TH AND WAS UNABLE TO FINISH IT BEFORE I LEFT. I ALSO HAD TAX PAPERWORK HANGING OVER MY HEAD LIKE A SPECTER. MY SISTER-IN-LAW, WHO HAD DONE ALL OF OUR BUSINESS PAPERWORK, INVOICING, AND TAX FILING RECENTLY LEFT AND THIS WAS THE FIRST TIME I WAS FILING BY MYSELF. IN FRANCE.

IT WAS EASY TO GET ACQUAINTED WITH EVERYONE. THERE WAS A MIX OF WRITERS AND VISUAL ARTISTS WITH MANY DIFFERENT BACKGROUNDS. I GOT INTO A ROUTINE QUICKLY TO BALANCE MY OBLIGATIONS WITH CREATING FOR MY TRAVELOGUE. WHICH YOU ARE READING NOW.

HOW META IS THAT?

WE UNPACKED AND STARTED SETTING UP OUR STUDIOS.

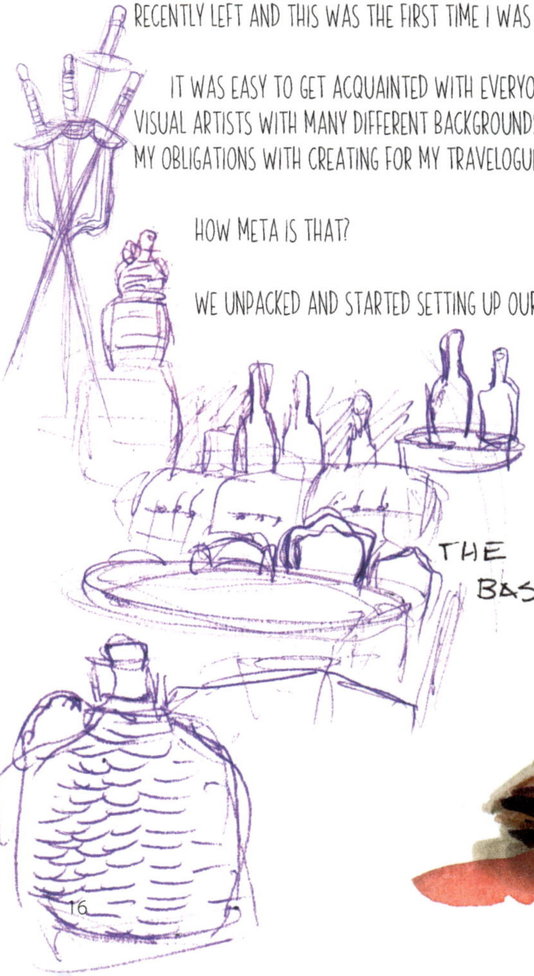

THE BASEMENT

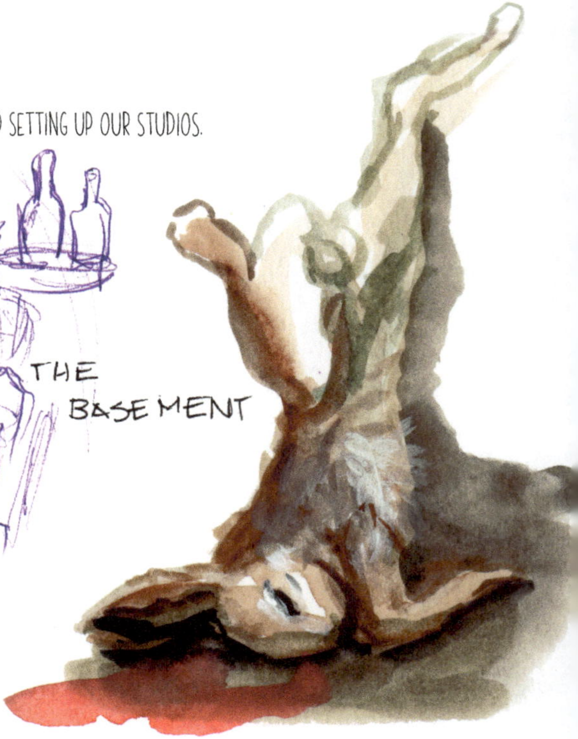

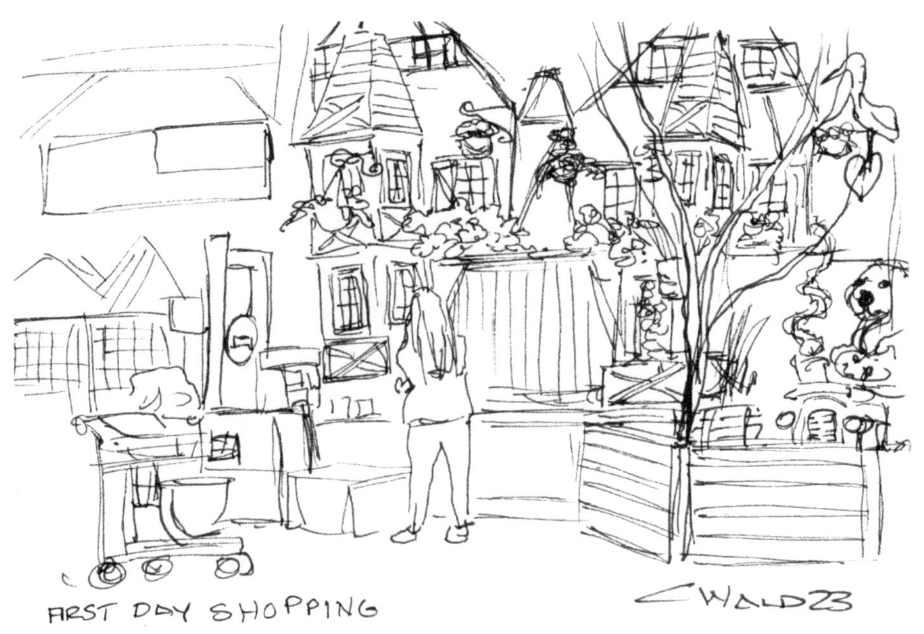

DAY 2

WE GOT A COMPREHENSIVE TOUR. THE HISTORY OF THE CHATEAU IS FASCINATING. IT WAS BUILT
AS A HUNTING CASTLE AND IS FILLED WITH HUNTING ORIENTED PAINTINGS, TAPESTRIES, AND
TAXIDERMY. MORE ON THAT LATER.

WE LEARNED THE INS AND OUTS OF DOING LAUNDRY, WHERE TO GO TO BE A LITTLE LOUDER LATE AT NIGHT, AND
WERE INTRODUCED TO THE WINE CAVE. THERE IS ALSO AN ART SUPPLY ROOM STOCKED WITH PAPER, PAINT, AND
MANY OTHER USUAL AND UNUSUAL SUPPLIES. MOST ARE LEFT BY PEOPLE WHO DO NOT WANT TO SHIP THEM AFTER
THE RESIDENCY.

THE FIRST FULL DAY, WE ALSO TOOK A FIELD TRIP TO AU COMPTOR DU JARDINIER, A GARDEN AND CRAFT STORE, TO
BUY ART SUPPLIES. WE ALSO WENT TO THE GROCERY STORE TO BUY ANY ESSENTIALS WE FORGOT, LIKE FLIP FLOPS
FOR THE SHOWER, AND WINE. ONE CANNOT FORGET THE WINE WHEN IN FRANCE AND THIS STORE HAD SO MANY
CHOICES!

I SPENT THE AFTERNOON SKETCHING THE STABLES, A FORMER EQUINE BUILDING NOW FILLED WITH ART STUDIOS
AND BATS. IT IS A BEAUTIFUL STRUCTURE. I FOUND A NICE SHADY SPOT AND SPENT A FEW HOURS ADMIRING IT.
THERE WERE APPARENTLY A LOT OF BATS LIVING IN THE ATTIC, BUT AFTER MY TRIP, THE BUILDING WAS RENOVATED
AND LEFT LITTLE SPACE FOR OUR WINGED FRIENDS.

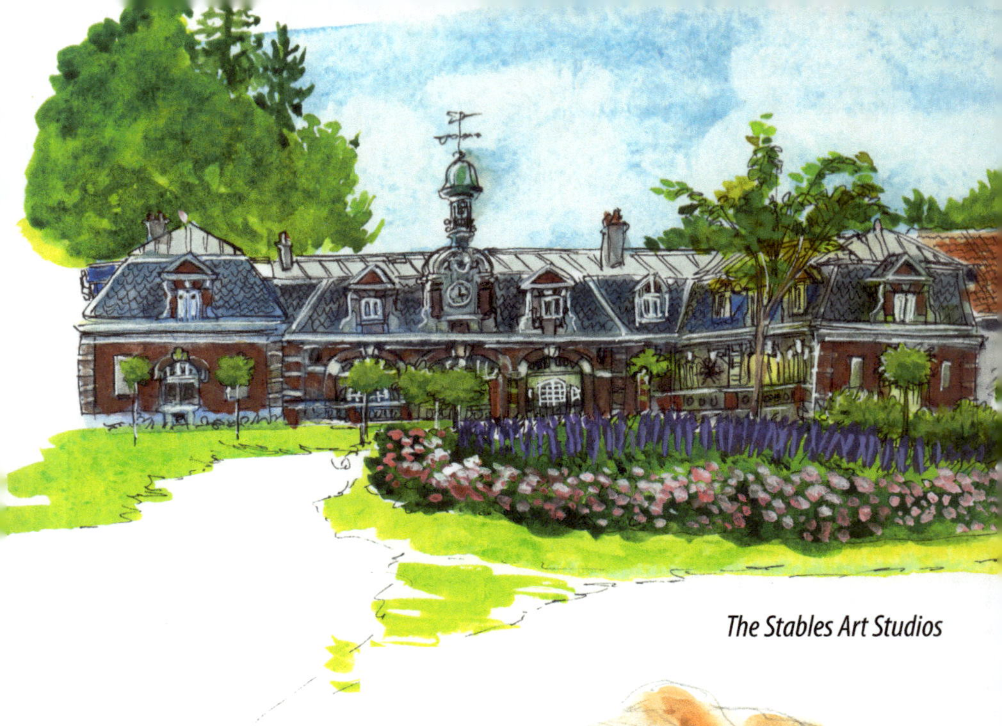

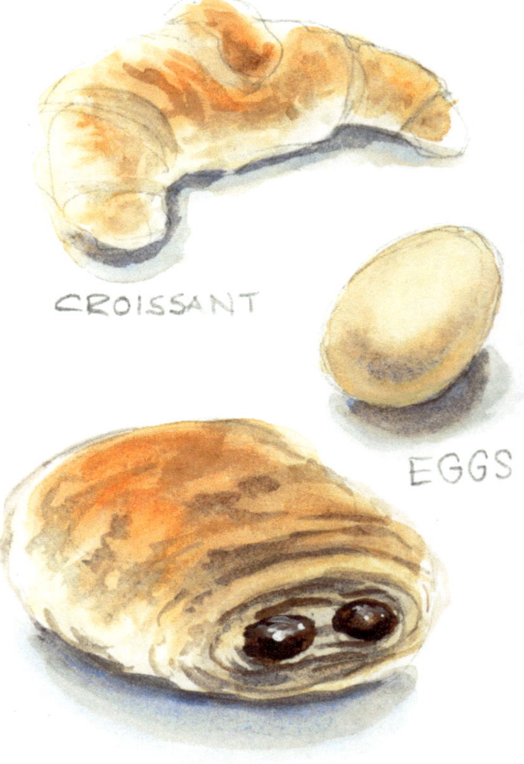

The Stables Art Studios

DAY 3

EACH MORNING BEGINS WITH A LOVELY BREAKFAST OF CROISSANTS (DELIVERED FROM THE NEIGHBORING VILLAGE OF POISSON), SLICED SALAMI, HARD-BOILED EGGS, FRUIT, AND COFFEE. THERE IS ALSO A DAILY SCHEDULE POSTED ON INSTAGRAM AND ON A BLACKBOARD IN THE ENTRYWAY WITH WRITING GROUPS AND VARIOUS CONSULTATIONS WITH BEULAH AND OTHER ARTISTS.

ROXY STARTED A MEDITATION CIRCLE WITH KAT, ONE OF THE WRITERS IN THE GROUP.

MY DAY STARTED WELL WHEN AN ILLUSTRATION FOR A BOOK I WAS WORKING ON BEFORE I LEFT WAS APPROVED.

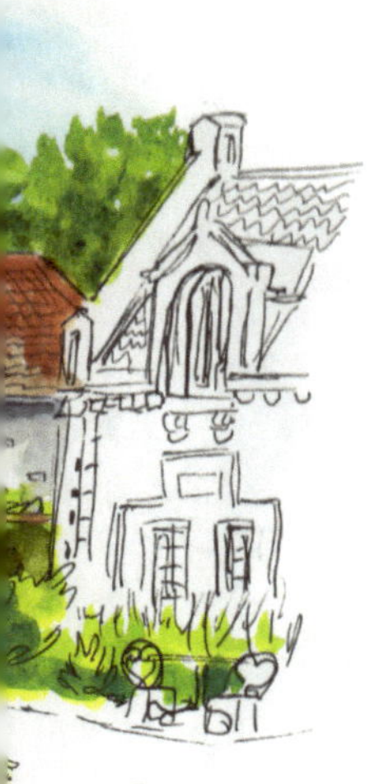

I CELEBRATED BY PAINTING A STREET SCENE FEATURING THE VILLAGE CASTLE ON THE HILL. I HAD BEEN OBSESSED WITH GOUACHE LATELY AND SPENT FOUR HOURS CAPTURING THE SCENE. IT TAKES LONGER THAN THE TYPICAL SKETCH. AND I AM STILL FEELING IT OUT AND DEVELOPING MY FAVORITE TECHNIQUES. THE SCANNER LOVES IT WHICH IS A REASON TO MASTER THE .MEDIUM. IT WAS NOT MY BEST PAINTING. BUT I ENJOYED CREATING IT.

AFTER DINNER. SHAWNA. A PAINTER CN THE RESIDENCY. RECRUITED PEOPLE TO MAKE A REEL USING AN OPENING DOOR VIDEO EFFECT. WE BROKE INTO THE COSTUME CAVE. PUT ON ALL SORTS OF HATS. ACCESSORIES. AND CLOTHES. SHE FILMED IN THE SALON AND ROXY DANCED AT THE CLOSING OF THE VIDEO. IT FELT ON POINT FOR THE SPIRIT OF THE CHATEAU.

THE EVENING ENDED IN A GHOST HUNT. ONE OF THE WRITERS. NIKI. BROUGHT AN EMF METER. A DEVICE USED BY GHOST HUNTERS TO DETECT THE PRESENCE OF SPIRITS. THE HOUSE DID NOT SEEM TO HAVE MUCH ACTIVITY. BUT THE METER LIT UP ON THE STAIRS AND THE BASEMENT. IT APPEARED THAT MOST OF THE ENTITIES SHARING THE SPACE WERE BENIGN. MORE ON THAT LATER TOO. EVERY PLACE YOU GO TELLS A STORY.

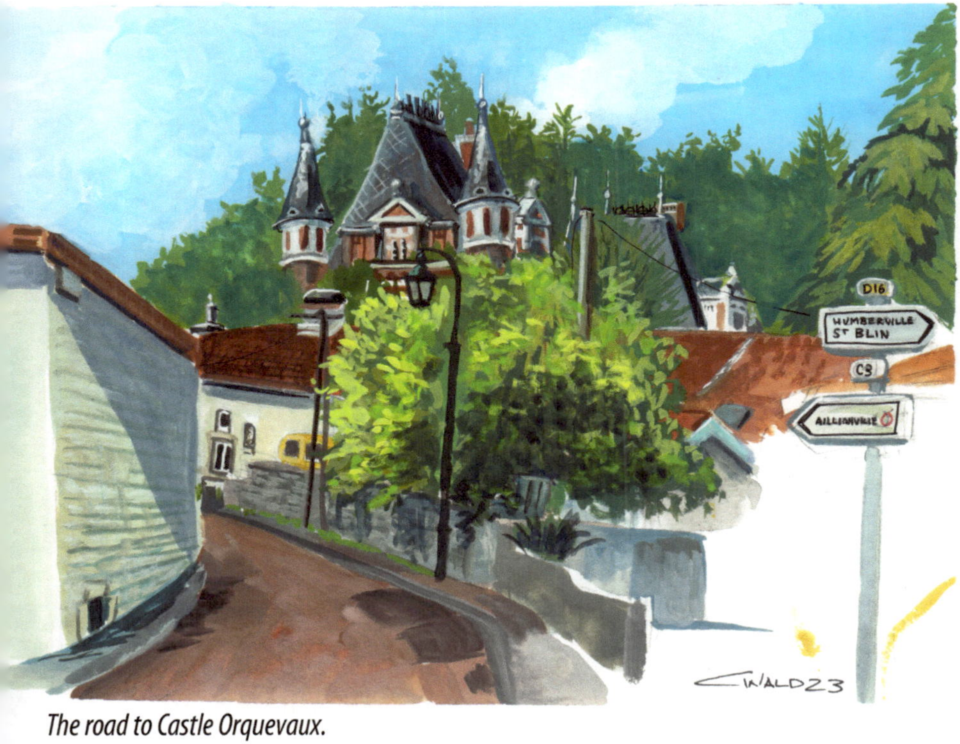

The road to Castle Orquevaux.

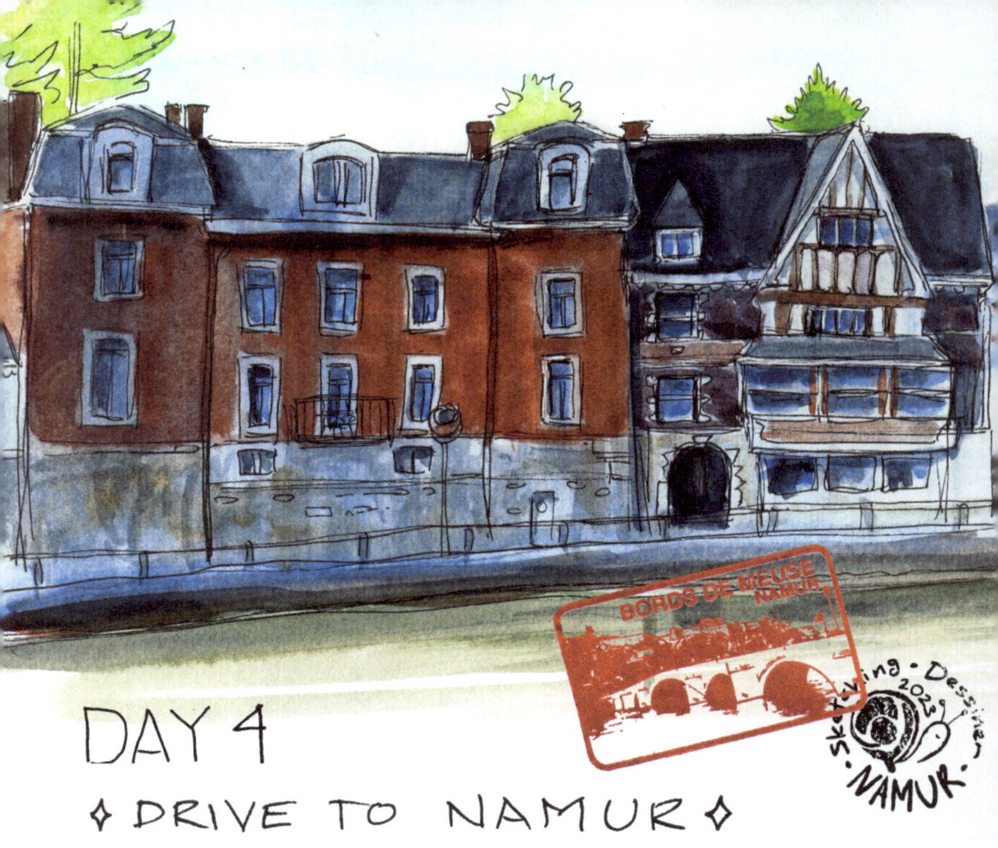

DAY 4
◊ DRIVE TO NAMUR ◊

UNEXPECTEDLY. THE DRIVE BECAME AN ADVENTURE.

FIRST. SOME BACKGROUND. I AM THE URBAN SKETCHERS SOCIAL MEDIA COORDINATOR. ONE OF THE BIG PROGRAMS WE RECENTLY STARTED IS AWARDING REGIONAL EVENT GRANTS SO PEOPLE IN DIFFERENT PARTS OF THE WORLD ARE ENCOURAGED TO DO THEIR OWN EVENTS IN ADDITION TO THE YEARLY SYMPOSIUM. I NOTICED ONE OF THE GRANT RECIPIENTS WAS IN NAMUR. BELGIUM DURING MY RESIDENCY AND WAS A THREE HOUR DRIVE AWAY FROM THE CHATEAU. THE ORGANIZER INVITED ME TO ATTEND AND SINCE I WAS IN FRANCE FOR A MONTH. I DECIDED TO CHECK IT OUT.

THE LANDSCAPE IN FRANCE IS EPIC! I DROVE ON NEARLY EMPTY RURAL ROADS THROUGH OCHRE ROLLING HILLS DOTTED WITH HAY BALES AND WINDMILLS. IT REMINDED ME OF THE PAINTINGS IN THE BOARDGAME **SCYTHE**.

TAKING IN THE BUCOLIC ATMOSPHERE WAS WONDERFUL UNTIL I GOT A FLASHING LIGHT ON THE DASHBOARD SAYING I NEEDED TO REPLENISH THE ADBLUE IN 100 KM.

WHEN WE RENTED THE CAR. I ASKED THE REPRESENTATIVE WHO DID OUR PAPERWORK IF WE NEEDED TO BE CONCERNED ABOUT IT WHEN I NOTICED THERE WAS A LIGHT ON THE DASH SAYING ADBLUE IN GLOWING LETTERS.

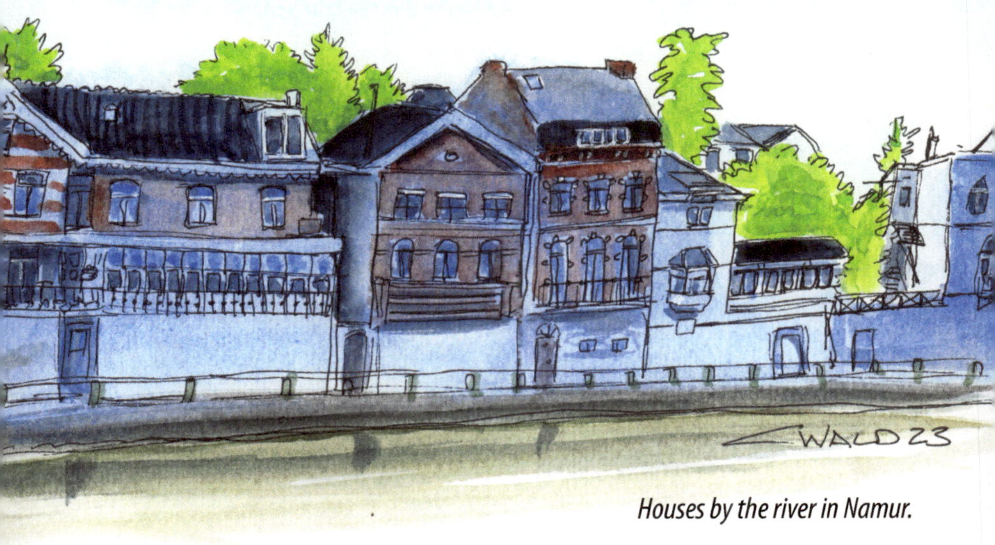

Houses by the river in Namur.

WHAT IS ADBLUE?" I ASKED.

"IT IS AN ADDITIVE TO A DIESEL EXHAUST THAT DOES NOT NEED TO BE FILLED VERY OFTEN. YOU WILL NOT HAVE TO THINK ABOUT IT." SHE SAID WITH EXTREME CONFIDENCE.

THE DRIVE WAS ALREADY FRAUGHT BECAUSE THE CREDIT CARDS AT THE TOLL BOOTH HAD TO BE CONTACTLESS. THERE WAS NO CHOP READER. FORTUNATELY, MY BACKUP CREDIT CARD I KEEP FOR EMERGENCIES WAS AND WORKED TO MY EXTREME RELIEF.

I PULLED OFF TO LOOK UP HOW TO GET ADBLUE. I TEXTED MY FRIEND IOANA, WHO RENTS DIESEL CARS IN ROMANIA ALL OF THE TIME, IF SHE HAD HEARD OF IT. NOPE. I CALLED ROXY. SHE ASKED AROUND AND WAS TOLD IT IS AN ADDITIVE TO MAKE DEISEL CAR EXHAUST CLEAN FOR THE ENVIRONMENT AND COULD BE PURCHASED AT SOME GAS STATIONS.

SO BEGAN MY SCAVENGER HUNT IN THE FRENCH COUNTRYSIDE TO FIND IT. AFTER SEVERAL STOPS, I FINALLY FOUND A GROCERY STORE THAT HAD GAS PUMP-LIKE DISPENSERS, AND A HELPFUL YOUNG MAN THAT SHOWED ME HOW TO PAY AND WORK THE MACHINE. SINCE COVID, GAS STATIONS HAVE NO ATTENDANTS. ONE BIG HELP WAS THAT MY USAA VISA CARD WOULD AUTOMATICALLY SHOW ALL THE TRANSACTION DETAILS IN ENGLISH. GOOGLE TRANSLATE ALSO HELPED.

I CHECKED INTO MY HOTEL AND HEADED OUT.

MY ADVENTURE MADE ME LATE TO THE FRIDAY NIGHT EVENT BUT I WAS STILL ABLE TO MEET THE GROUP FOR PIZZA. NAMUR IS SITUATED ON A SCENIC RIVER. IT WAS PLEASANT TO MEET THE SKETCHERS RUNNING THE EVENT AND SKETCH THE SUNSET. I ALSO GOT TO MEET LUDI. WHO I HAVE WORKED WITH THROUGH URBAN SKETCHERS FOR YEARS ON VARIOUS PROJECTS. LIKE OUR QUARANTINE PODCAST USK TALKS. BUT NEVER MET IN PERSON.

THE DINNER WAS VERY LONG SINCE THE PIZZA PLACE WAS SLAMMED WITH NUMEROUS ORDERS. WHICH MEANT MORE TIME TO CHAT AND VISIT WITH THE GROUP

I TALKED AT LENGTH WITH ONE OF THE ORGANIZER'S DAUGHTERS. ZOE. I NOTICED SHE WAS READING PATTI SMITH'S BOOK **JUST KIDS**. A GOOD BUT UNUSUAL CHOICE FOR A YOUNG PERSON. WE DISCUSSED OUR FAVORITE PODCASTS AND SHE CONFIDED ABOUT SOME OF HER PERSONAL PARANORMAL EXPERIENCES. HER FATHER IN ADDITION TO BEING AN URBAN SKETCHER. TAUGHT COMICS AT THE ART SCHOOL IN TOWN. BELGIUM IS WELL-KNOW FOR HERGE. THE MASTERMIND BEHIND **TIN TIN**.

I WALKED BACK TO THE HOTEL WITH A SKETCHER WHOSE DAY JOB IS COMPUTER PROGRAMMING AND WE CHATTED ABOUT BELGIUMS DIFRFERENT SKETCHING EVENTS.

DAY 5

❦ A DAY OF SKETCHING ❦

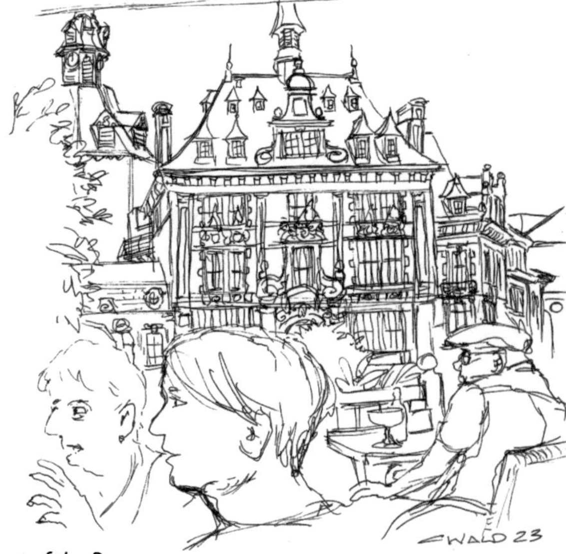

Sketching in front of the Bourse.

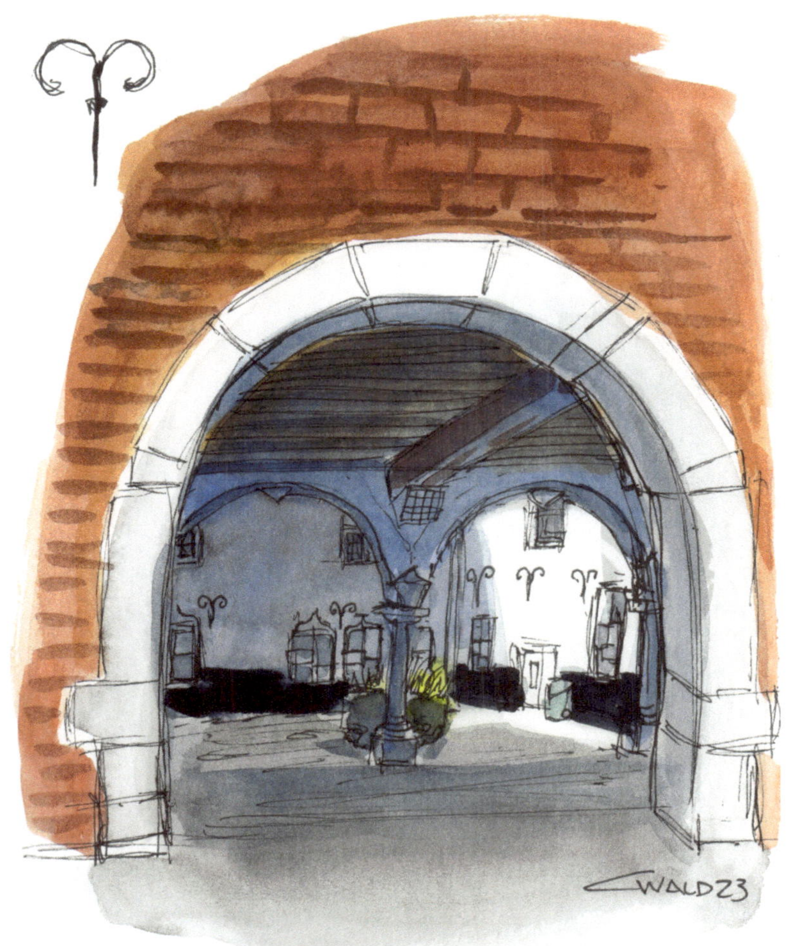

ACADÉME DES BEAUX-ARTS

THERE WAS A LONG LINE AT CHECK-IN. THIS WAS A FREE EVENT OF SKETCH WALKS AND DEMOS.

AFTER I GOT MY GOODIE BAG AND STAMPS, I WENT TO A CAFE BY THE BOURSE, A GOVERNMENT BUILDING, TO SKETCH WITH SOME NEW AND OLD FRIENDS. THE CAFE WAS A FUN PLACE FOR PEOPLE WATCHING. ONE WOMAN I SKETCHED LOOKED LIKE MY MOTHER-IN-LAW. THE NAMUR EVENT ALSO HAD LOCAL CULTURE DEMOS WHICH WERE VERY INTERESTING. I LOVE SEEING OLD FOLK TRADITIONS OF DIFFERENT COUNTRIES AND VILLAGES.

A SKETCH WALK TO AN OLD TANNERY TURNED INTO AN ART SCHOOL WAS HELD THAT AFTERNOON. IT WAS IN FACT THE ART SCHOOL WHERE BENOIT, ONE OF THE EVENT ORGANIZERS, TEACHES DRAWING COMICS THE BELGIAN WAY. I LOVE HOW THE BUILDING WAS REFITTED TO BE AN EDUCATION CENTER BUT STILL RETAINED CLASSICAL CHARM. THERE WAS A GRASSY PATIO AREA WITH SOME EXCELLENT SKETCHING VANTAGE POINTS.

♈ DINNER IN NAMUR ♈

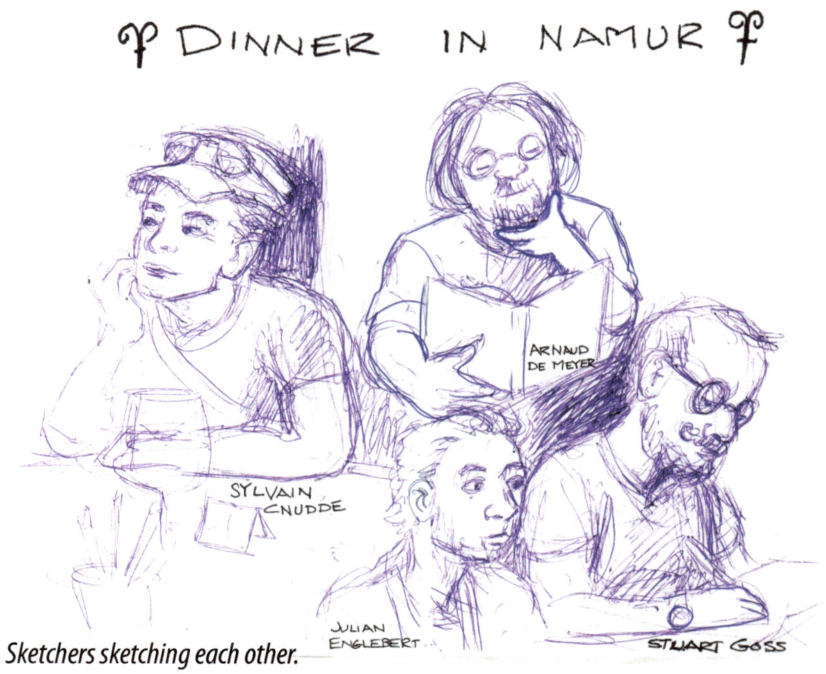

Sketchers sketching each other.

THAT EVENING, WE HAD A BEAUTIFUL DINNER AT LA BOURSE DE NAMUR ON THE TOP FLOOR. MANY PEOPLE TOOK THEIR DINNERS TO THE PATIO SINCE THE VENUE WAS NOT AIR-CONDITIONED. THE BEST PART OF THE EVENING WAS EVERYONE DREW ON THE TABLECLOTHS. IT WAS EXCITING TO BE WITH A GROUP OF LIKE-MINDED, SKETCHING OBSESSED PEOPLE.

I FOUND OUT THAT I WAS THE ONLY AMERICAN AT THE EVENT. EVERYONE WAS TALKING ABOUT THE SKETCH WALK PLANNED FOR BERLIN IN THE FOLLOWING SEPTEMBER THAT ALREADY HAD OVER 1000 PEOPLE SIGNED UP!

SADLY, I HAD TO SAY GOODBYE TO EVERONE SINCE I PLANNED TO GET OUT EARLY THE NEXT MORNING AND HEAD BACK TO THE CHATEAU.

DAY 6

I GOT UP EARLY TO SKETCH THE HOMES ON THE WATER BEFORE I LEFT. THE MORNING LIGHT WAS INCREDIBLE. I ALSO HAD TO GET A PHOTO WITH LUDI BEFORE I LEFT TO SHOW TO OUR USK TALKS CREW.

THE DRIVE BACK WAS VERY QUIET. WHY IS IT THAT THE GAS STATION ONE ALWAYS PICKS IS MORE EXPENSIVE THAN THE NEXT PLACE YOU PASS? I WAS STILL FEELING OUT HOW 'EMPTY' THE CAR COULD GET. I PASSED ONE STATION

THINKING THE NEXT WOULD BE CLOSE AND
THEN PANICKING WHEN I COULD NOT FIND
ONE LATER. OF COURSE. AFTER I FILLED UP,
THERE WERE MULTIPLE STATIONS CLOSE AND
CHEAPER. I SUPPOSE IT IS SOME TYPE OF
TRAVELER LAW.

ROXY HAD ASKED THAT I STOP AT A GROCERY
STORE FOR SOME WINE ON THE WAY HOME.
LITTLE DID I KNOW THAT NOTHING IS OPEN ON
SUNDAYS. THE CLOSEST I CAME WAS AN ALDI
WHICH HAD CLOSED AT NOON MINUTES BEFORE I
ARRIVED. SO, AFTER SEVERAL STOPS, I CAME BACK
EMPTY-HANDED.

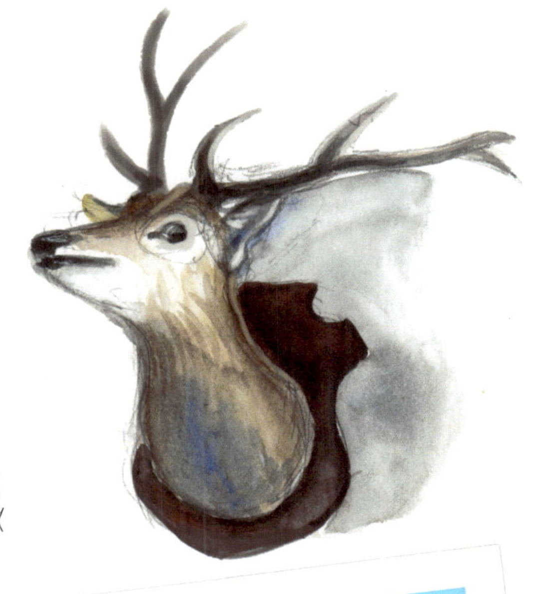

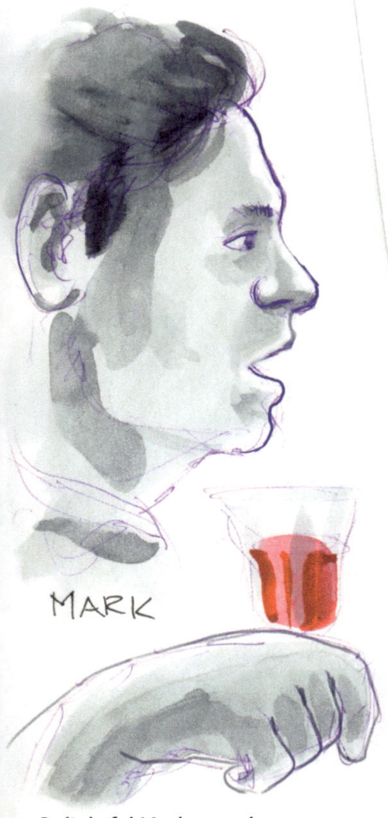

Delightful Mark monologue.

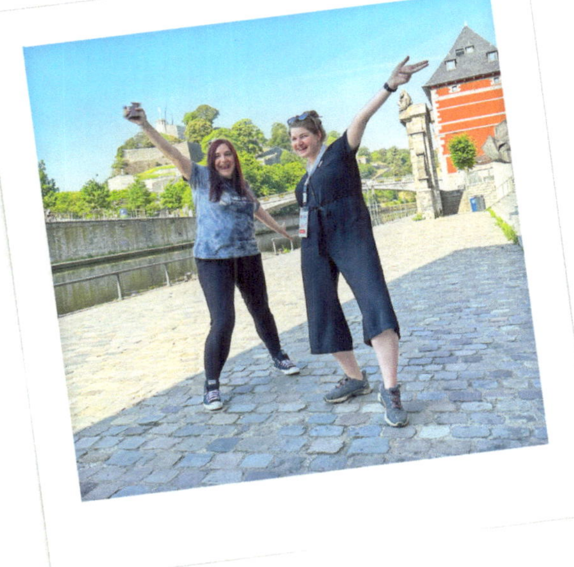

I finally met Ludi in person.

I GOT BACK TO THE CHATEAU IN THE LATE AFTERNOON AND WE
HAD A PLEASANT BOOZY EVENING. WITH MARK LEADING WITH
LIVELY STORIES. I ALSO WORKED ON A BOOK COVER I WAS TRYING
TO FINISH. THE WEEKENDS ARE INTERESTING AT THE CHATEAU.
IT IS FAIRLY QUIET THE FIRST WEEKEND AFTER ARRIVAL. AND A
WHIRLWIND DURING OPEN STUDIO.

DAY 7

SO MUCH HAPPENED THIS MONDAY!

ROXY AND I DROVE TO SKETCH THE SUNFLOWER FIELDS.

WE PARKED ON THE SIDE OF THE ROAD AND SET UP FOR A COU-
PLE OF HOURS. THE FLOWERS ACTUALLY TURNED AS WE PAINTED.
IN FACT, THEY ARE CALLED TOURNESOL IN FRENCH. WE WERE
ONLY INTERRUPTED BY THE VERY OCCASIONAL VEHICLE INCLUDING
GIANT TRACTORS. BEES BUZZED AND BUTTERFLIES FLITTED
AROUND US. THE NUMEROUS WINDMILLS CAST INTERESTING
SHADOWS AROUND US.

IT WAS MAGICAL.

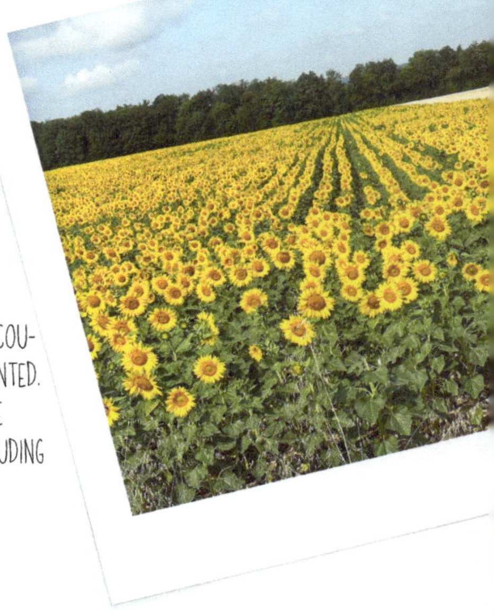

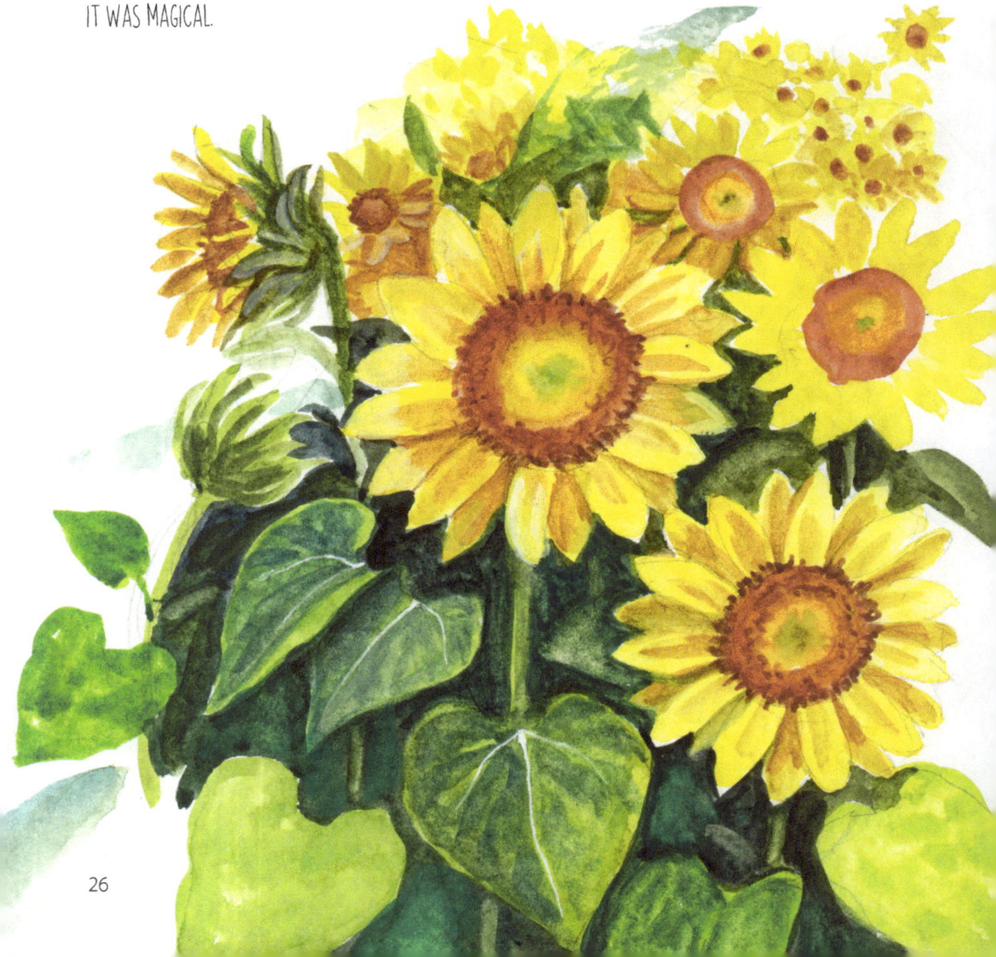

POETRY READING

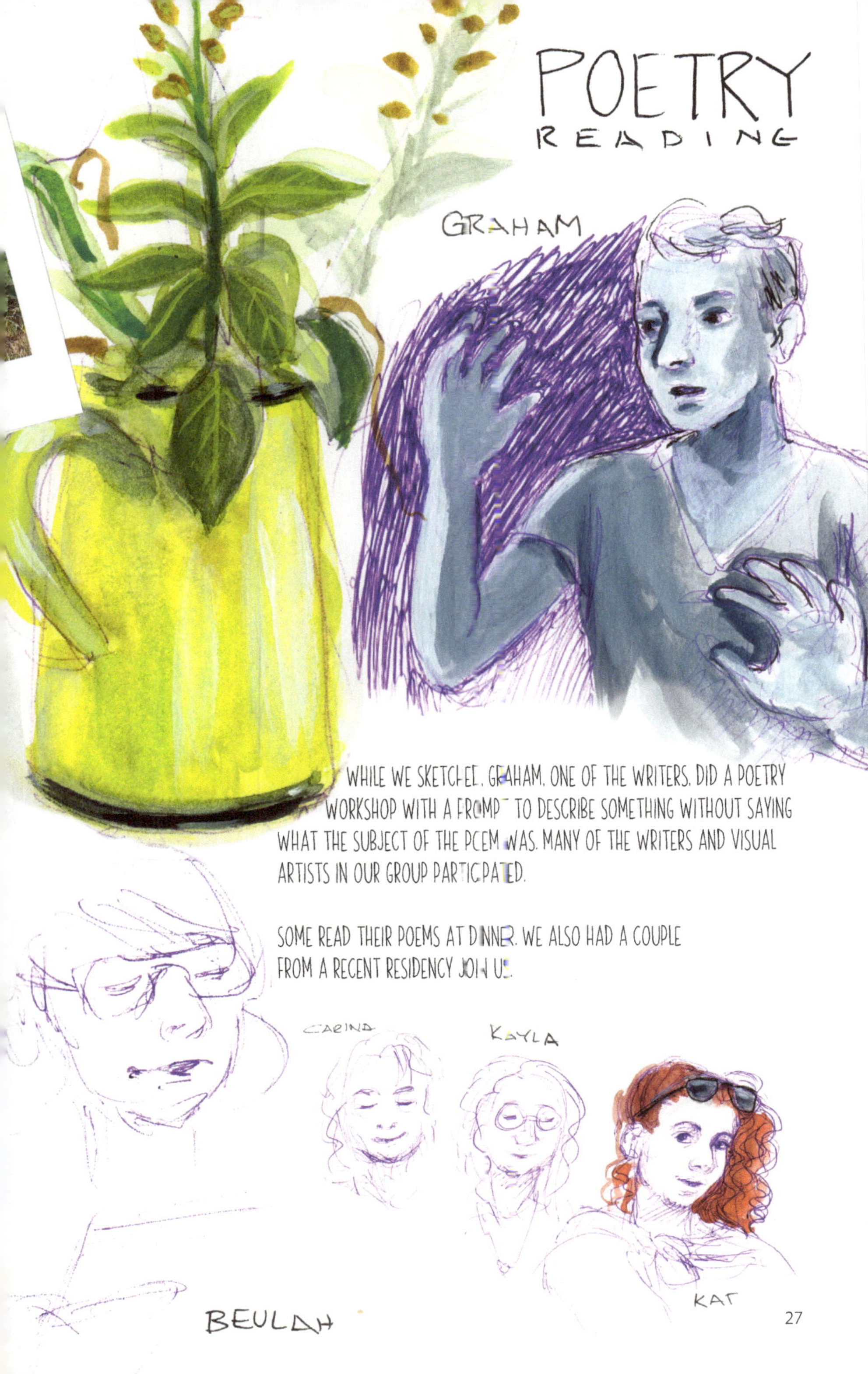

WHILE WE SKETCHED, GRAHAM, ONE OF THE WRITERS, DID A POETRY WORKSHOP WITH A PROMPT TO DESCRIBE SOMETHING WITHOUT SAYING WHAT THE SUBJECT OF THE POEM WAS. MANY OF THE WRITERS AND VISUAL ARTISTS IN OUR GROUP PARTICIPATED.

SOME READ THEIR POEMS AT DINNER. WE ALSO HAD A COUPLE FROM A RECENT RESIDENCY JOIN US.

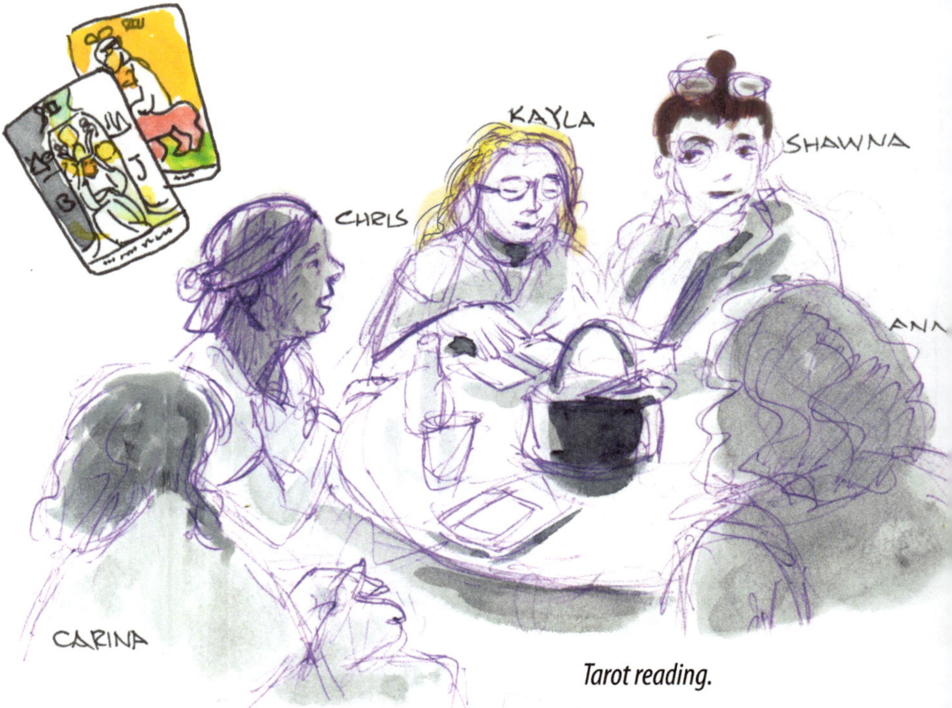

Tarot reading.

SHAWNA ASKED KAYLA, ANOTHER WRITER AND PAINTER, TO DO A TAROT READING FOR HER. IT BROKE THE ICE AND EVERYONE WANTED ONE. SHE AGREED TO GIVE ALL WHO WANTED IT A THREE CARD READING. EVEN THE PREVIOUS RESIDENCY GUESTS WERE INTERESTED.

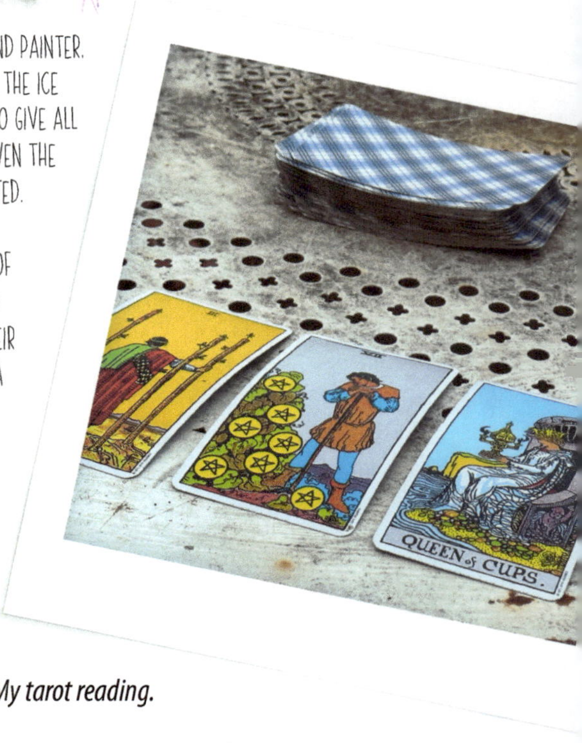

KAYLA PATIENTLY DISCUSSED THE MEANING OF EVERYONE'S CARDS. IT IS ALWAYS A WAY TO LEARN ABOUT EVERYONE WHEN YOU SEE THEIR INTERPRETATION OF THE CARDS. MY THREE, A THREE OF WANDS, A SEVEN OF PENTACLES, AND THE QUEEN OF CUPS. IT SEEMED TO BODE WELL.

IT ALSO TURNS OUT THAT ONE OF THE GUESTS WAS FROM CLEVELAND, OHIO. NO MATTER WHERE YOU GO IN THE WORLD, PEOPLE HAVE TIES TO OHIO.

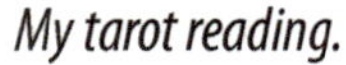

My tarot reading.

IT IS A NEXUS.

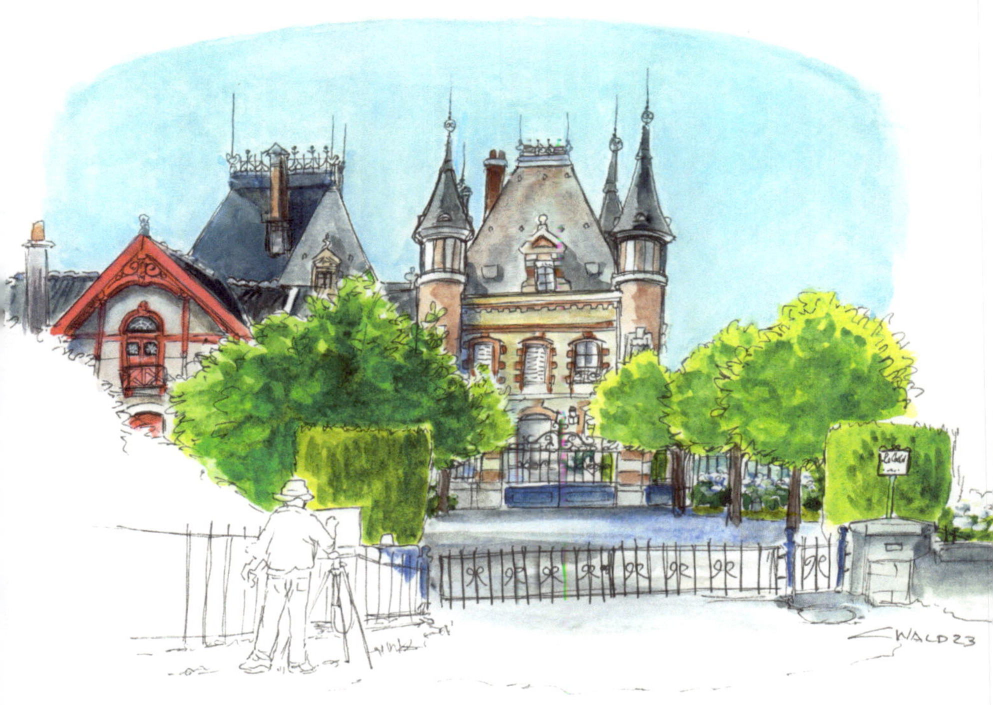

DAY 8

GREG, ROXY, AND I GOT UP VERY EARLY TO SKETCH THE VILLAGE CASTLE. I HAVE A BIT OF A CASTLE OBSESSION SO I WAS EAGER TO SKETCH IT FROM A DIFFERENT ANGLE. THE CASTLE DOMINATES FROM THE TOP OF THE HILL. THE CHURCH ACTUALLY USED TO BE THERE BUT A PREVIOUS OWNER OF THE CHATEAU HAD IT MOVED TO BUILD THE CASTLE FOR HIS 'MISTRESS'. THAT IS WHY THERE IS A STAIRWAY UP TO AN OLD GRAVEYARD. ON THE PROPERTY. THE CASTLE IS NOW AN AIR B&B.

WE WERE INVITED BY ONE OF THE CARETAKERS. WHO WAS CLEANING THE INSIDE, TO LOOK AROUND THE GROUNDS. I WAS STILL PAINTING SO ROXY WENT IN AND TOOK PHOTOS. THE GROUNDS ARE SIMPLY GORGEOUS! THERE IS A LITTLE ORCHARD AT THE STREET ENTRANCE AND SOME INTERESTING SCULPTURE INCLUDING A BUCK WHICH ROXY DID A PAINTING OF. I WOULD LOVE TO GET A TOUR OF THE INSIDE.

THE DAY OR TWO BEFORE. WE WERE TOLD THERE WOULD BE A LITERATURE SALON. SINCE THE CHATEAU USED TO BE INHABITED BY ART CRITIC, WRITER, AND PHILOSOPHER. DENIS DIDEROT. IT IS FITTING TO BE A PART OF THE RESIDENCY. ZIGGY CAME UP WITH THE IDEA FOR EACH PERSON TO READ A QUOTE OR PASSAGE BY SOMEONE WHO INSPIRES THEM OR THAT THEY HAVE WRITTEN.

IT WAS SO INTERESTING TO SEE WHAT PEOPLE CHOSE TO SHARE.

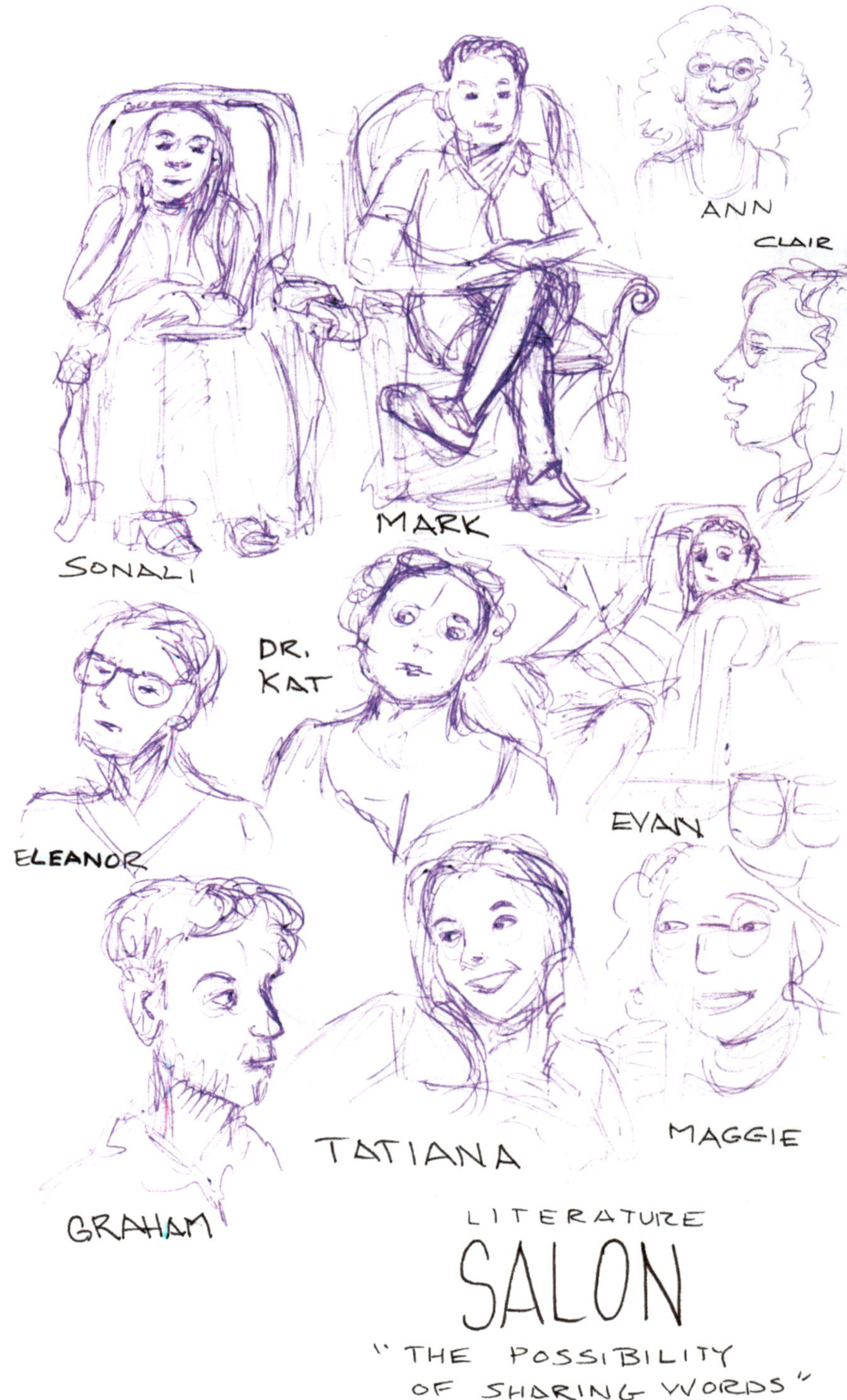

ANN
CLAIR
SONALI
MARK
DR. KAT
ELEANOR
EVAN
GRAHAM
TATIANA
MAGGIE
LITERATURE
SALON
" THE POSSIBILITY
OF SHARING WORDS "

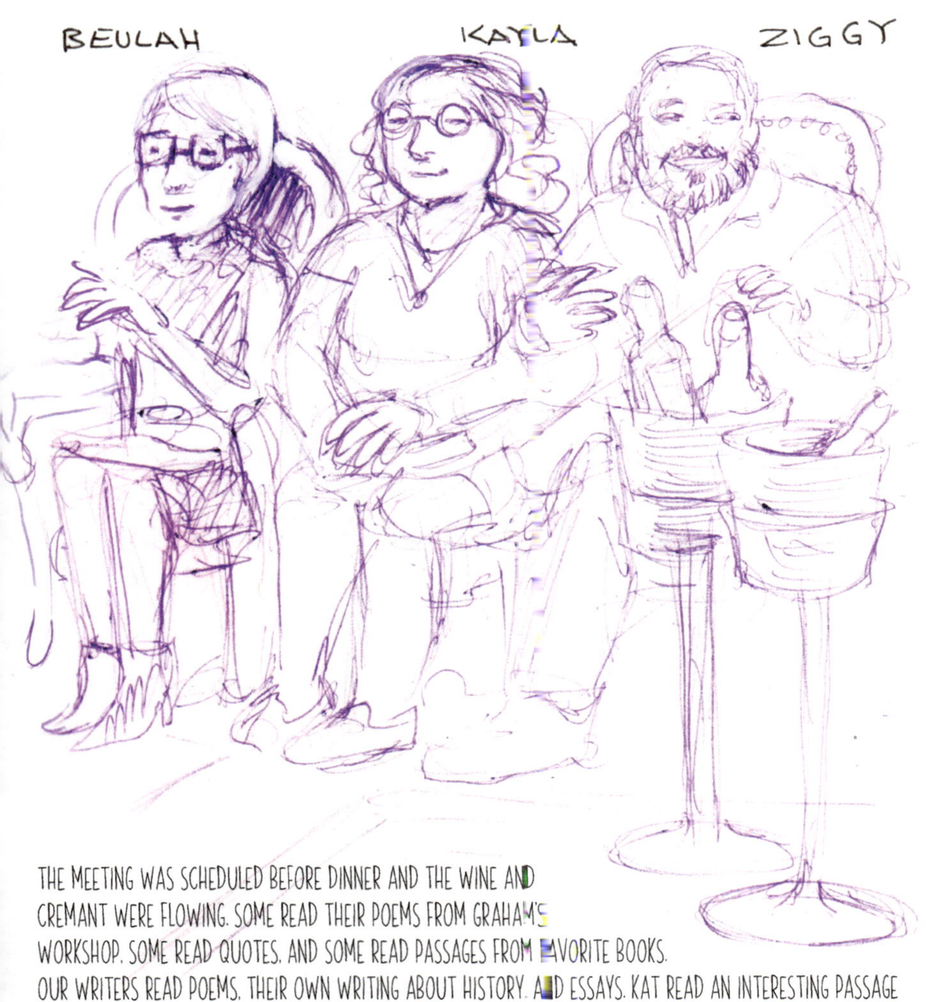

THE MEETING WAS SCHEDULED BEFORE DINNER AND THE WINE AND CREMANT WERE FLOWING. SOME READ THEIR POEMS FROM GRAHAM'S WORKSHOP. SOME READ QUOTES. AND SOME READ PASSAGES FROM FAVORITE BOOKS. OUR WRITERS READ POEMS. THEIR OWN WRITING ABOUT HISTORY. AND ESSAYS. KAT READ AN INTERESTING PASSAGE FROM THE BOOK SHE WAS FINISHING. ZIGGY READ THE POEM THAT STARTS THIS TRAVELOGUE.

I READ A GEORGIA O'KEEFFE QUOTE THAT WAS IN MY SKETCHBOOK AND IS AT THE BEGINNING OF THIS TRAVELOGUE. I HAVE RECENTLY BEEN DOING MORE WRITING AND KIND OF WISH I HAD WRITTEN SOMETHING.

ROXY HAD BEULAH READ HER EMOTIONAL LETTER TO HER DAUGHTERS SINCE SHE WAS UNCOMFORTABLE SPEAKING DUE TO HER SPASMODIC DYSPHONIA.

IT WAS A VALUABLE LEARNING EXPERIENCE AND BROUGHT THE GROUP CLOSER TOGETHER. THERE IS SOMETHING PROFOUND ABOUT THAT SORT OF SHARING.

DAY 9

THE DAY STARTED WITH A SEMINAR ABOUT THE ART BUSINESS WITH BEULAH. SHE IS HEAVILY INVOLVED IN THE GALLERY MARKET. I HAVE BEEN IN A LOT OF SHOWS. BUT SINCE I AM AN ILLUSTRATOR. I HAVE NEVER DONE A DEEP DIVE INTO THAT MARKET.

THE ART WORLD IS ALWAYS CHANGING DUE TO SO MANY EXTERNAL FORCES. I THOUGHT SHE HAD A LOT OF GOOD ADVICE ESPECIALLY ABOUT CONTACTING GALLERIES AND USING LINKTREE AS A TOOL.

THE RESIDENCY ATTENDEES ARE IN ALL STAGES OF THEIR ART CAREERS. WE HAVE A LOT TO LEARN FROM EACH OTHER AND AS AN EDUCATOR.

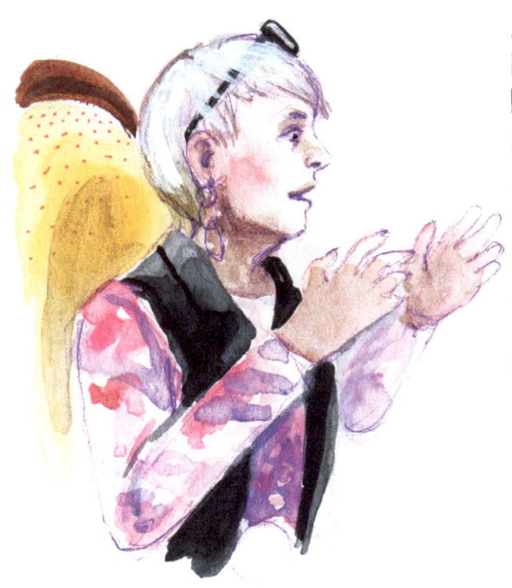

Beulah dropping knowledge.

I ALWAYS FIND HEARING OTHER EXPERIENCES FASCINATING AND USEFUL IN MY PRACTICE.

DUSTY SUDDENLY APPEARED AT THE HOUSE AFTER BEING KEPT INDOORS AT ZIGGY AND BEULAH'S HOUSE NEXT TO THE STABLES. HE IS A YOUNG CAT BUT FEELS COMFORTABLE IN HIS PRINCELY DOMAIN. HE ABSORBED SO MUCH ATTENTION AT THE BUSINESS DISCUSSION AND LATER. HE SLEPT IN THE CHAIR IN ROXY'S STUDIO FOR A FEW HOURS.

THE REST OF THE DAY WAS IN THE STUDIO. I AM STILL STRUGGLING WITH FINISHING THE BOOK COVER SO I CAN GET TO CREATING MORE ARTWORK IN THIS BEAUTIFUL ENVIRONMENT. WE ALSO PLANNED AN EXCURSION TO DIJON TOMORROW. I WAS LAST THERE IN 2018 SO I AM REALLY EXCITED TO VISIT AGAIN.

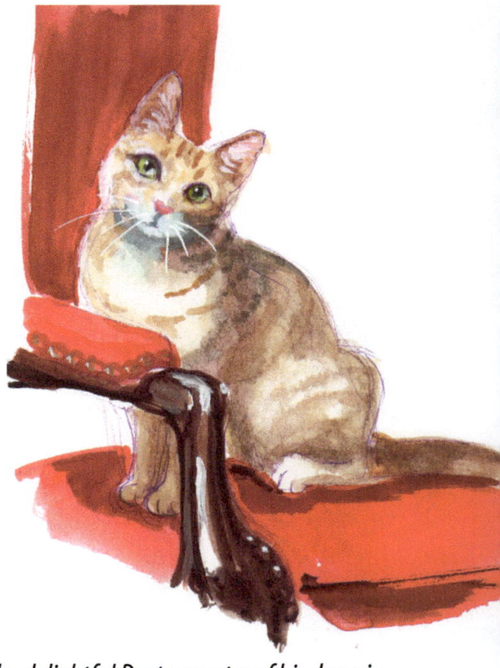

The delightful Dusty, master of his domain.

DAY 10

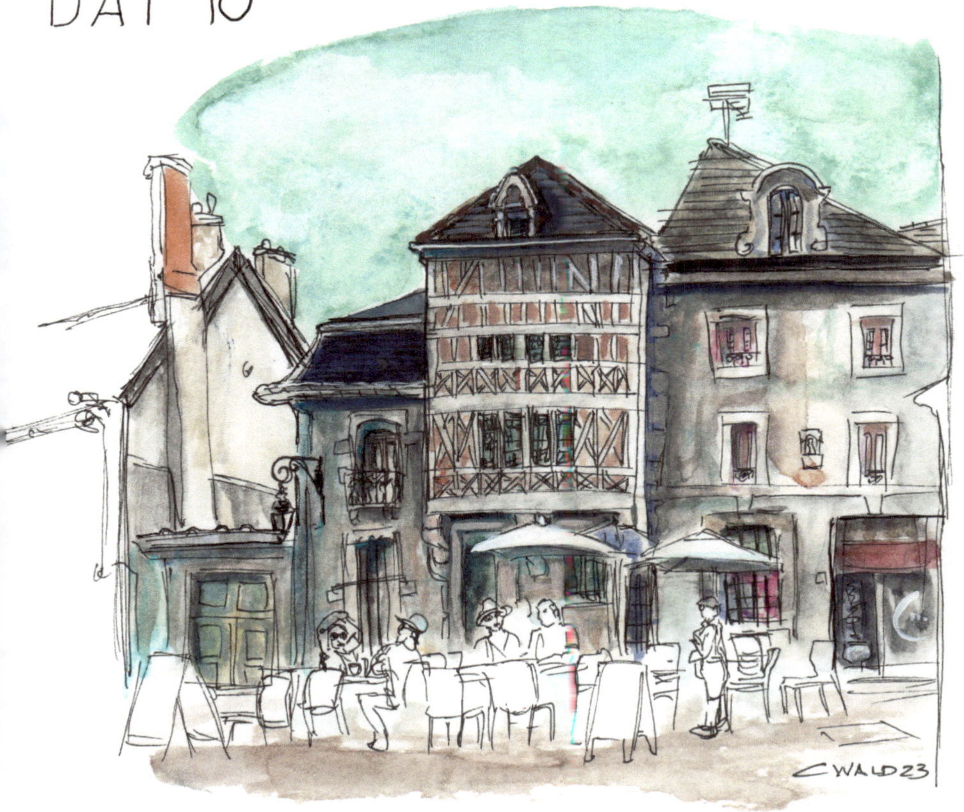

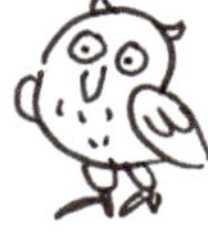 DAY IN DIJON

SINCE WE HAD A CAR, WE DECIDED TO TAKE A FEW SIDE TRIPS. WE FIGURED OUT A SHORT LIST BEFORE WE LEFT.

DIJON IS A BIT OVER ONE AND A HALF HOURS AWAY AND IS THE CAPITAL CITY OF THE BURGUNDY WINE REGION. I VISITED THERE IN 2018 AND STAYED FOR A FEW DAYS. I LOOKED FORWARD TO VISITING AGAIN AND MY **SKETCHING HERE & EVERYWHERE** BOOK COVER FEATURED A BUILDING I SKETCHED THERE. ROXY DROVE CLAIR, GREG AND MYSELF TO THE OLD TOWN AREA.

OF COURSE, A CAR MEANS PARKING AND THE FIRST THING WE HAD TO FIGURE OUT WAS WHERE TO PARK AND HOW TO PAY FOR IT. ONCE AGAIN, HELPFUL YOUNG PEOPLE CAME TO THE RESCUE AND SHOWED US HOW TO PAY. THERE WERE KIOSKS IN FRENCH OR AN APP. WE WENT WITH THE KIOSK. THAT FINALLY SETTLED, WE WENT TO THE NOTRE-DAME CATHEDRAL IN TOWN WITH SOME OF THE MOST INTERESTING SCULPTURES ON ITS FACADE.

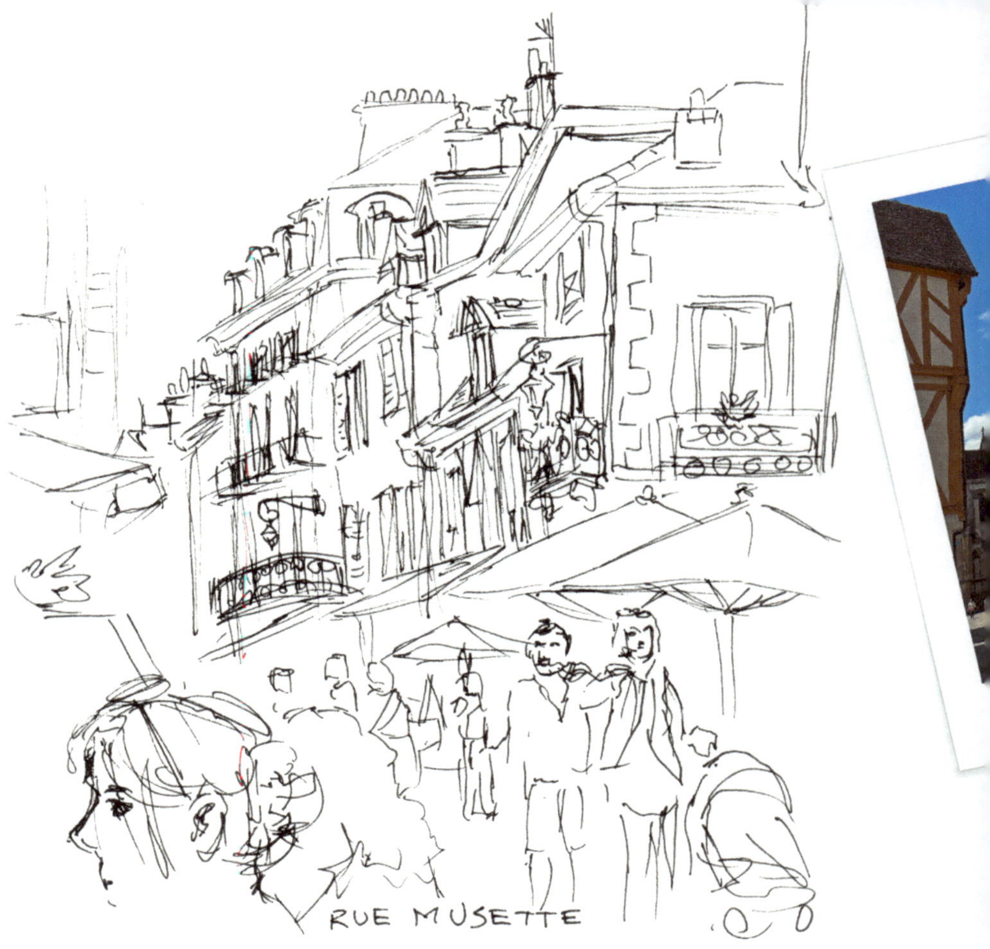

WE HAD LUNCH AT BOUILLON NOTRE-DAME. GREG GOT HIS FIRST TASTE OF ESCARGOT. I HAD STEAK FRITES AND THEN SKETCHED THE LIVELY STREET SCENE. A LOT OF THE OLD TOWN AREA IS CAR FREE SO IT FELT TIMELESS.

WE SEPARATED AFTER LUNCH TO EXPLORE AND IN MY CASE. SKETCH. I FOUND A NICE LITTLE NOOK WITH MORE OF THE FRENCH NORMANDY STYLE OF ARCHITECTURE. WE ALSO WANDERED AROUND AND TOOK PHOTOS. SADLY THERE WAS NOT TIME FOR THE MUSEE DES BEAUX-ARTS OR A WINE TASTING BEFORE OUR PARKING RAN OUT.

I MADE MY WAY TO HÔTEL AUBRIOT THE 13TH CENTURY BUILDING I HAD SKETCHED IN 2018. IT WAS RESTORED IN 1908 AND IN 2023 WAS A LITTLE WORSE FOR WARE BUT WAS STILL THERE IN ALL ITS GLORY. I FEEL LIKE I COULD LIVE IN THIS CITY. I LOVE THE ARCHITECTURE AND THEY HAVE A GREAT GAME STORE I WENT TO MY LAST VISIT. THEY INVITED ME TO COME TO A GAME NIGHT AND I BOUGHT A TRAVEL EDITION OF THE GAME **CASTLES OF BURGUNDY** IN BURGUNDY.

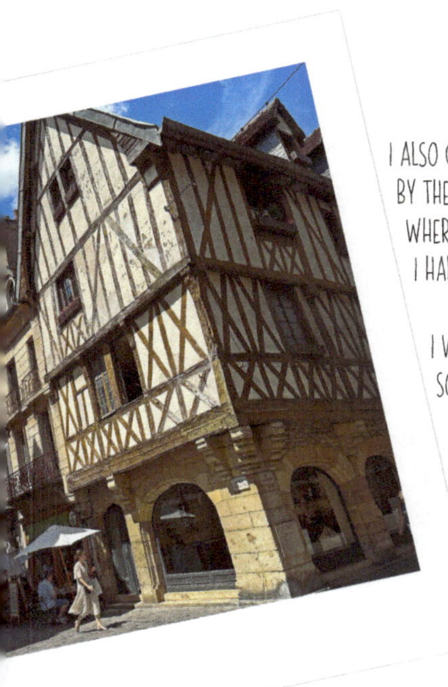

I ALSO CAPTURED A STREET SCENE THAT ALMOST LOOKED LIKE A CLICHÉ BY THE HOTEL WHERE I HAD SKETCHED. THERE WAS A FLOWER SHOP WHERE A MOTHER WAS SHOPPING WITH HER DAUGHTERS IN SUN HATS. I HAD TO PAINT IT

I WAS SAD TO LEAVE. I DROVE OUR CREW BACK TO THE CHATEAU SO WE WOULD ARRIVE FOR DINNER ON TIME.

WE HAD MISSED A LIFE DRAWING SESSION BUT GOT TO MEET THE SPIRITED PHOTOGRAPHER AND HIS MODEL AT DINNER. HE SHOWED US MANY PHOTOS OF HIS SESSIONS AT THE CHATEAU. I WAS SAD TO MISS AN OPPORTUNITY FOR LIFE DRAWING BUT FORTUNATELY THERE WOULD BE ANOTHER IN A WEEK OR SO.

Hôtel Aubriot, where I sketched my book cover.

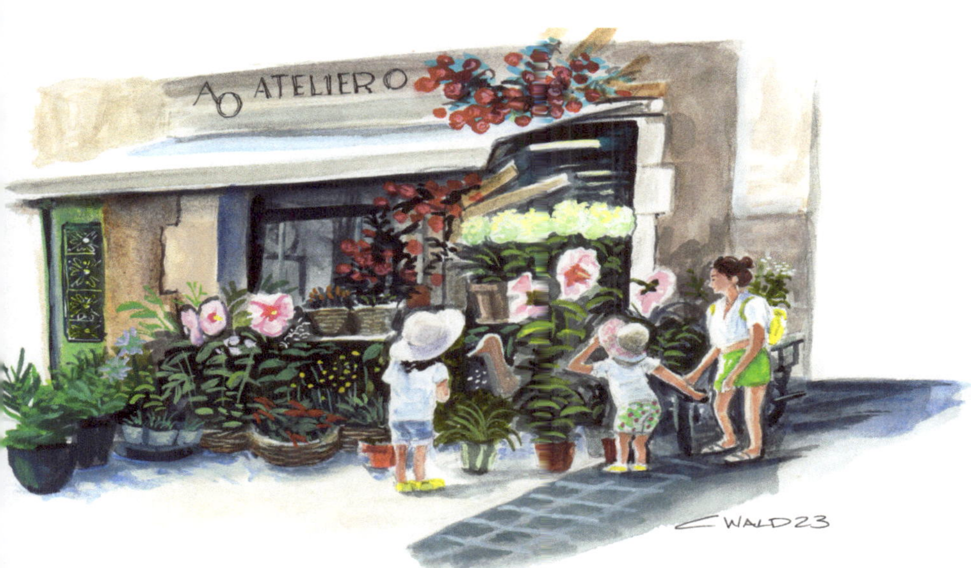

Who could resist sketching this scene.

DAY 11

IT IS A FRANTIC DAY OF PREPARATION! OPEN STUDIO IS TOMORROW!

EVERY TWO WEEKS, THE RESIDENT ARTISTS SHARE THE WORK THEY PRODUCED IN THERE STUDIO. SINCE I AM THERE FOUR WEEKS,

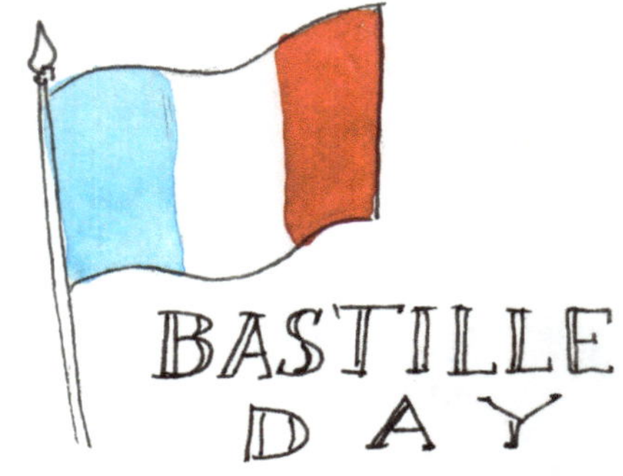

I GET THE OPPORTUNITY TO PARTICIPATE TWICE IN OPEN STUDIOS. THERE IS NO PRESSURE TO MAKE A BUNCH OF WORK BUT IT IS A WAY TO SHARE EVERYONE'S PRACTICE. I DID A COUPLE MORE PAINTINGS AND PREPARED TO DISCUSS MY TRAVELOGUE. WE ACTUALLY GOT A PREVIEW OF THE OPEN STUDIO THIS EVENING. LORI IS LEAVING EARLY SATURDAY TO SPEND A FEW EXTRA DAYS IN PARIS AND BOOK A FEW VENUES FOR A JAZZ MUSICIAN SHE MANAGES. SHE COLLAGES BUTTERFLY WINGS SHE GETS FROM THE SMITHSONIAN AND MAKES PORTRAITS. IN THIS CASE, IT WAS OF A FORGOTTEN ACTRESS. IT WAS AMAZING! SHE HAS THE DISTINCTION OF HAVING HER TECHNIQUE RIPPED OFF BY DAMIEN HIRST. THERE'S EVEN A BOOK ABOUT IT.

IT WAS ALSO ROXY'S BIRTHDAY! THEY PREPARED SOME SPECIAL CAKES AND I GOT HER A BOTTLE OF SPARKLING WINE. THE PARTY WENT LATE EVEN THOUGH I EXCUSED MYSELF TO WORK ON MY PRESENTATION INTO THE WEE HOURS.

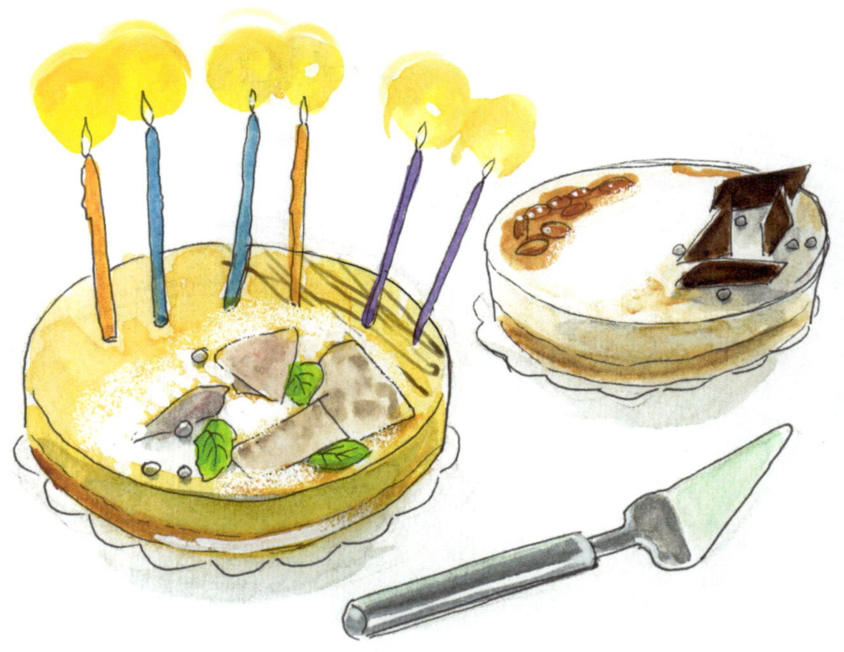

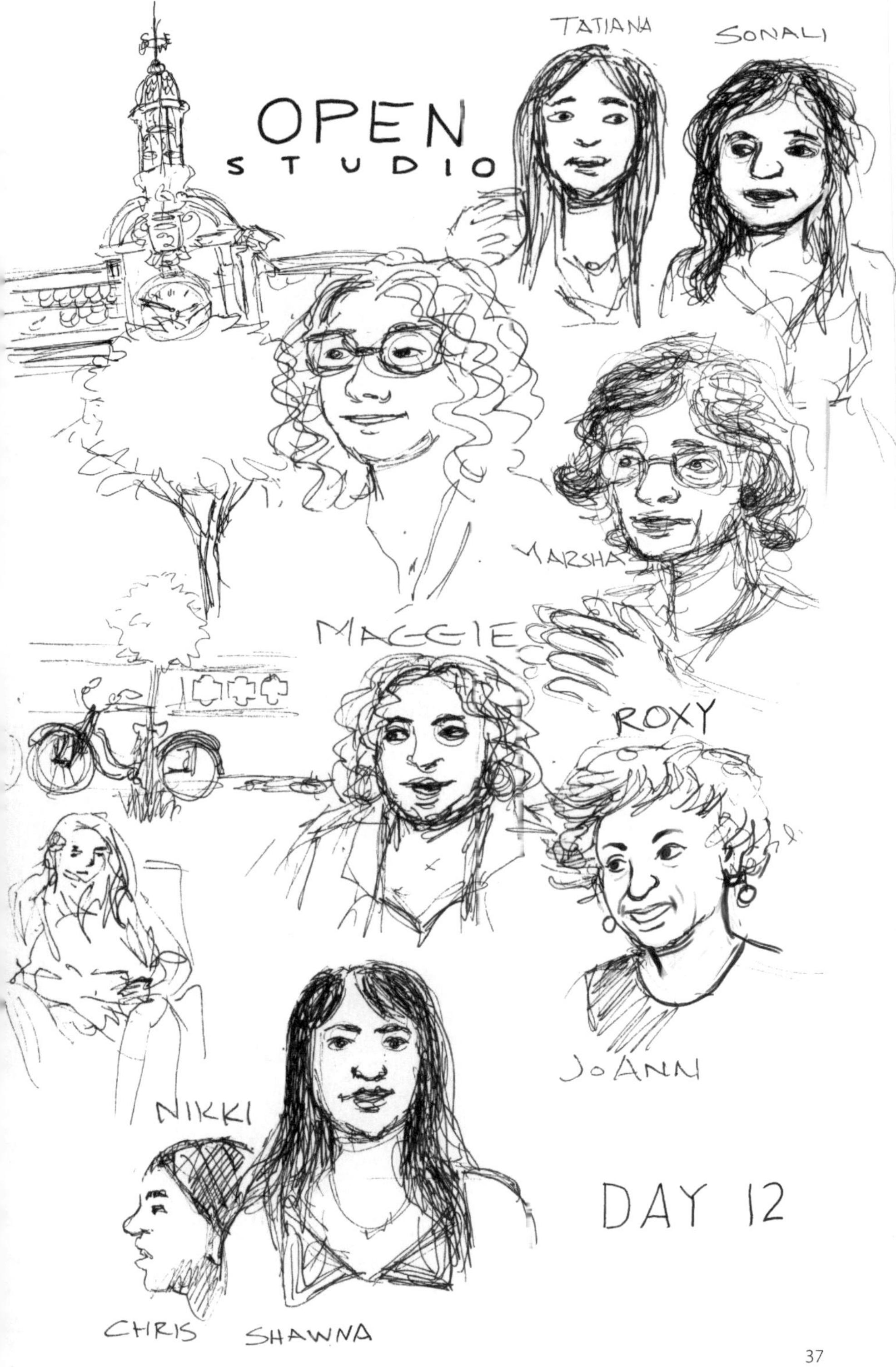

OPEN STUDIO
TATIANA
SONALI
MARSHA
MAGGIE
ROXY
JoANN
NIKKI
CHRIS
SHAWNA
DAY 12

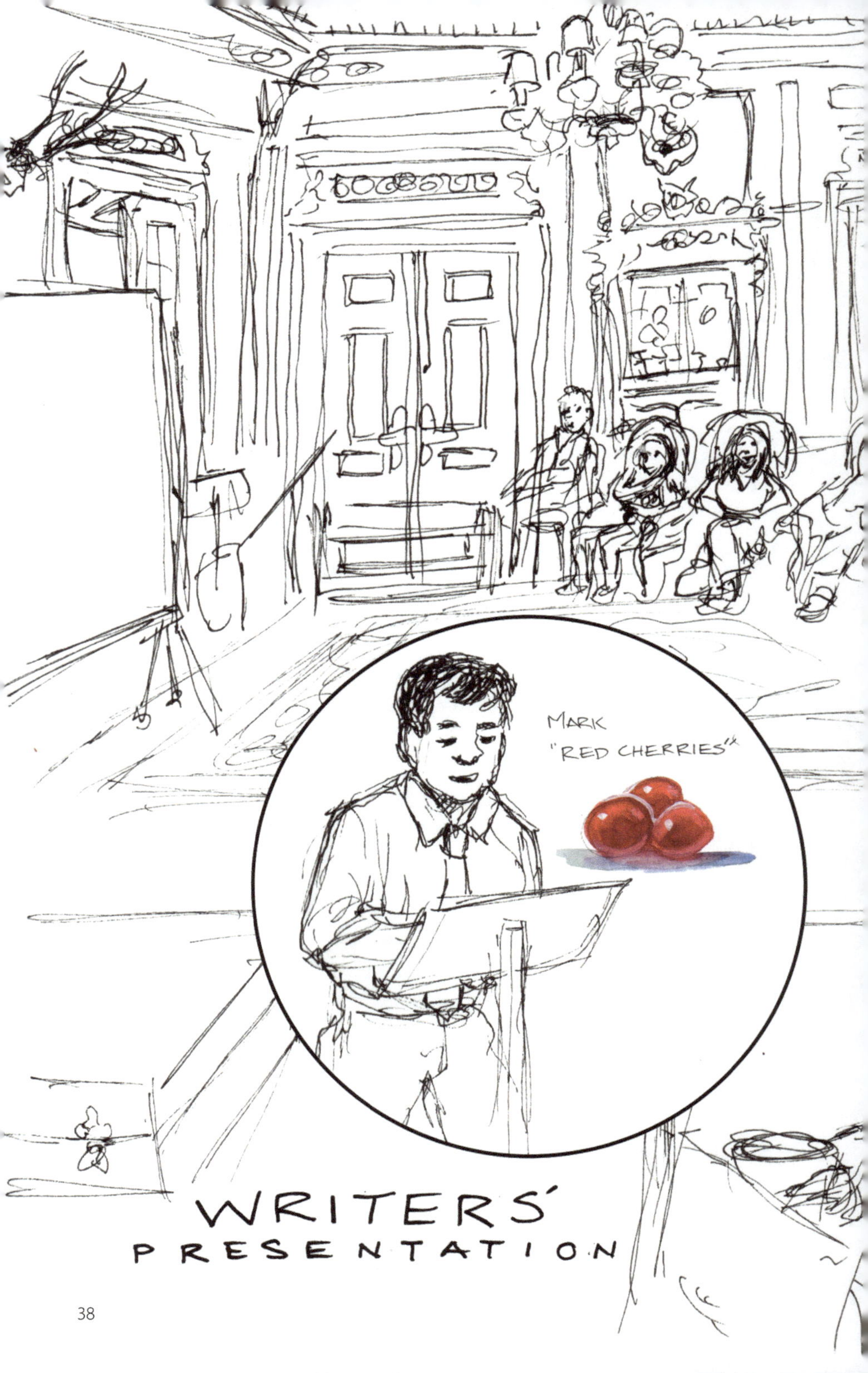

MARK
"RED CHERRIES"
WRITERS'
PRESENTATION
38

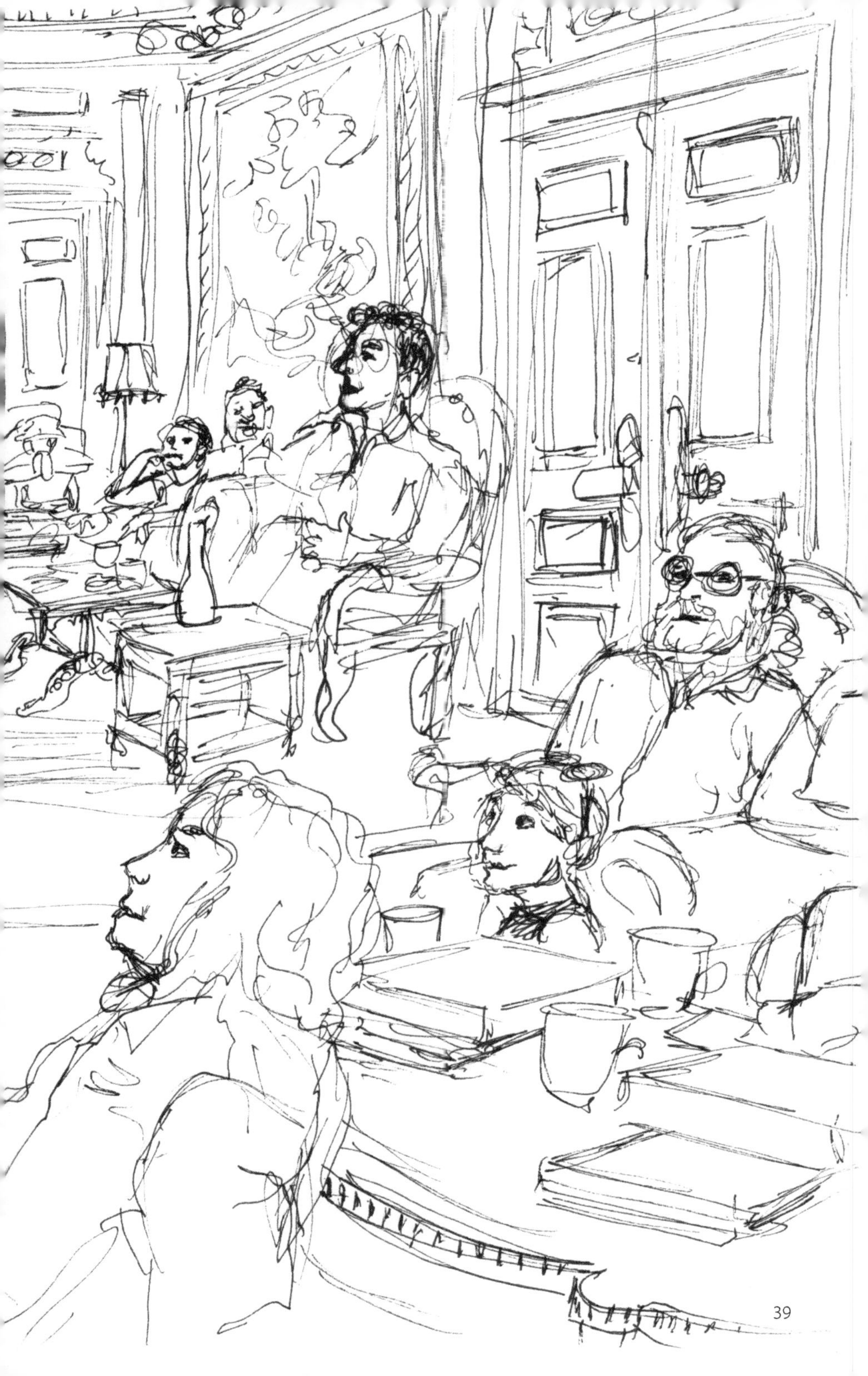

IT WAS SO EXCITING TO SEE EVERYONE'S WORK!

MARK READ A LOVELY AUTOBIOGRAPHICAL ESSAY ABOUT SOUR CHERRIES WHICH IS A COMMON MEMORY FROM THE MIDWEST. I HAD NOT THOUGHT ABOUT THEM FOR YEARS BUT THEY USED TO BE MY FAVORITE CANDY. THERE WAS REPRESENTATIONAL AND NON REPRESENTATIONAL WORK, SCULPTURE, COLLAGE, AND PAINTING EXPERIMENTS. ROXY, AFTER GETTING ENCOURAGEMENT FROM THE GROUP, GAVE A WONDERFUL PRESENTATION OF HER WORK. SHE PREPARED A FEW SKETCHES FOR PAINTING BEFORE WE LEFT AND SKETCHED WITH ME AS WELL.

I DID A PREVIEW OF THE TRAVELOGUE. NOTHING CONCRETE BUT THE INCEPTION.

IT WAS ALSO THE FINAL STUDIO WALK FOR CARINA. SHE HAD ARRIVED IN APRIL AND STAYED TO HELP OUT. SHE COORDINATED, MADE SURE THERE WERE ALWAYS FRESH FLOWERS, AND PLAYED MUSIC.
SHE IS AN AMAZING PAINTER AND IT WAS EXCITING
TO SEE HER WORK.

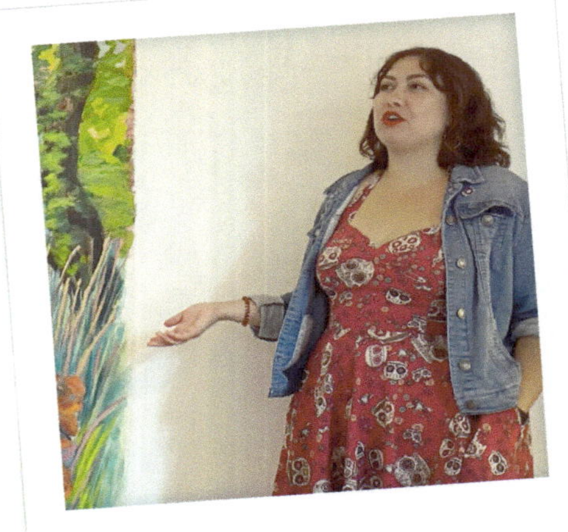

Carina's last studio walk of 2023.

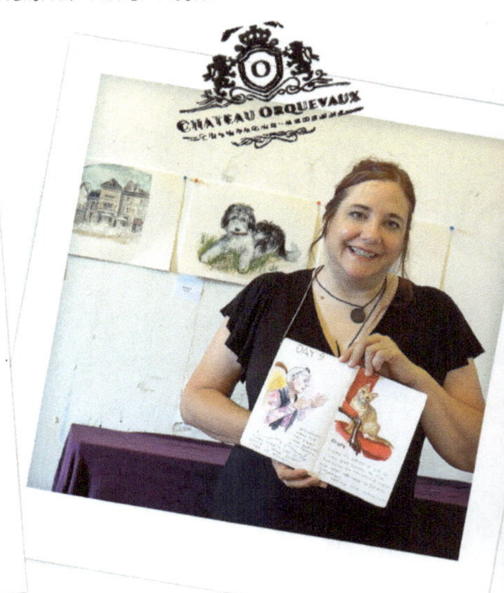

My presentation.

THE DAY ENDED WITH A DANCE PARTY OUTSIDE. BIG SPEAKERS WERE POSITIONED ON THE PORCH FOR THE DANCE TUNES. IT WAS A BIG RELEASE AFTER THE FRANTIC PACE.

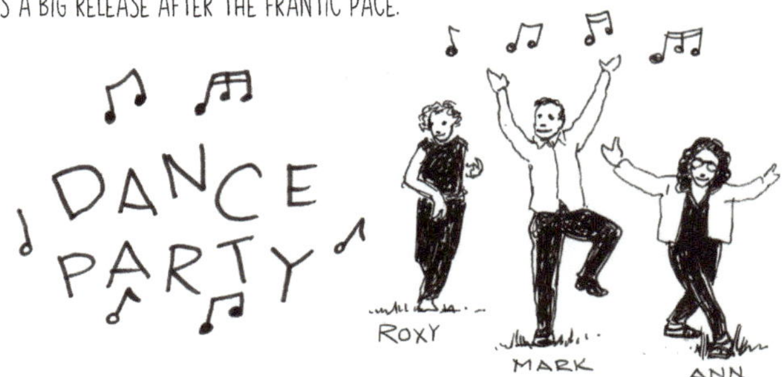

DAY 13

IT WAS THE BITTERSWEET LAST DAY OF THE RESIDENCY FOR EVERYONE BUT KAT, GREG, EVAN, AND ME.

BEFORE DINNER, THERE WAS A GATHERING WHERE EVERYONE EXPRESSED WHAT THE RESIDENCY MEANT TO THEM. IT WAS VERY EMOTIONAL. THIS IS A RARE TIME WHERE EVERYONE TAKES MEALS TOGETHER AND INTERACT IN A WAY THAT IS MORE IN-PERSON THAN MANY ARE USED TO.

THERE WAS ALSO THE FLURRY OF PACKING AND CLEANING OUT OF STUDIOS.
I WAS RELIEVED NOT TO HAVE TO WORRY ABOUT IT, THIS TIME.

DAY 14

EVERYONE HAD TO BE OUT BY NOON EXCEPT FOR THE MONTH-LONG RESIDENTS.

SINCE ROXY FLIES OUT TOMORROW, WE DECIDED TO STAY IN REIMS FOR A DAY.

IT DID NOT DISAPPOINT! WE CHECKED INTO OUR HOTEL AND SKETCHED AT THE FORMIDABLE CATHEDRAL THAT USED TO BE THE SEAT OF THE CATHOLIC CHURCH. FIRST, WE HAD A LUNCH BY SUBÉ FOUNTAIN.

NEXT WE CHECKED OUT THE SHOPS AND THE ARCHITECTURE. THE SALES ASSISTANT AT A HIGH-END GLASSES SHOP ADMIRED ROXY'S TASTE IN GLASSES. A TRUE FASHION DESIGNER TO THE CORE. HERS CAME FROM A WELL-KNOWN DESIGNER I HAD NOT HEARD OF SINCE I AM NOT IN THE KNOW OF EYE-WEAR DESIGN.

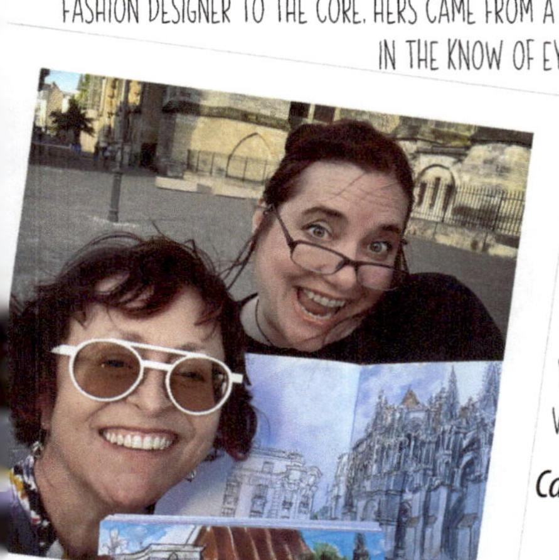

ROXIE SCOUTED OUT A MOROCCAN RESTAURANT FOR DINNER CALLED LE RIAD. WE ASKED IF WE COULD EAT OUTSIDE SINCE IT WAS A BEAUTIFUL EVENING AND WE WERE TOLD "NO!" BY THE STAFF, WHO SEEMED VERY OVERWORKED AND UNDERSTAFFED. WE SPLIT A TAGINE AND HAD A PLEASANT DISCUSSION WITH A DUTCH COUPLE. THE MAN REGALED US WITH HIS MMA FIGHT STORIES.

Cathedral selfie.

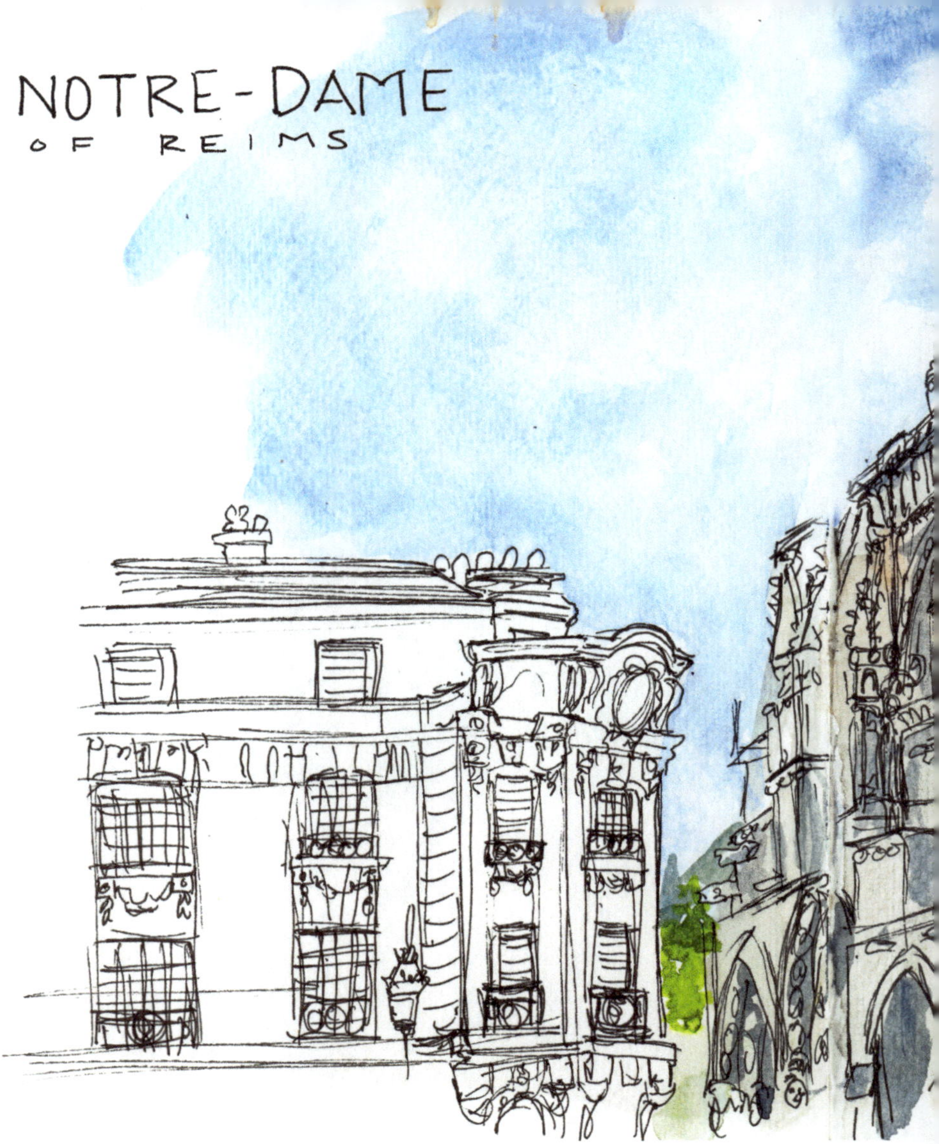

NOTRE-DAME
OF REIMS

DAY 15

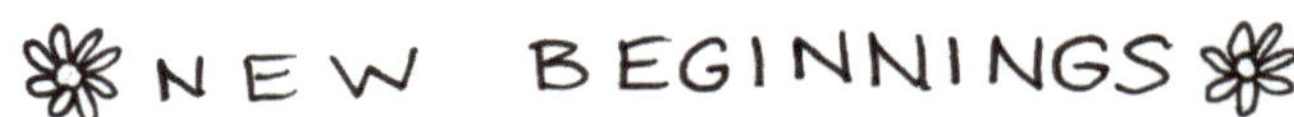

I DROVE ROXY TO THE AIRPORT AND DROVE BACK, LISTENING TO MICHAEL PALIN'S AUTOBIOGRAPHY ON AUDIBLE.

THE CHATEAU IS A HIVE OF ACTIVITY BETWEEN SESSIONS. BEDDING IS CHANGED. THE PROPERTY IS CLEANED, AND ACCOMMODATIONS PREPARED FOR THE NEW ARTISTS. I HAD FINALLY FINISHED MY BOOK COVER AND HEADED TO THE CREEK TO SKETCH FOR A WHILE UNTIL THE NEW RESIDENTS ARRIVED.

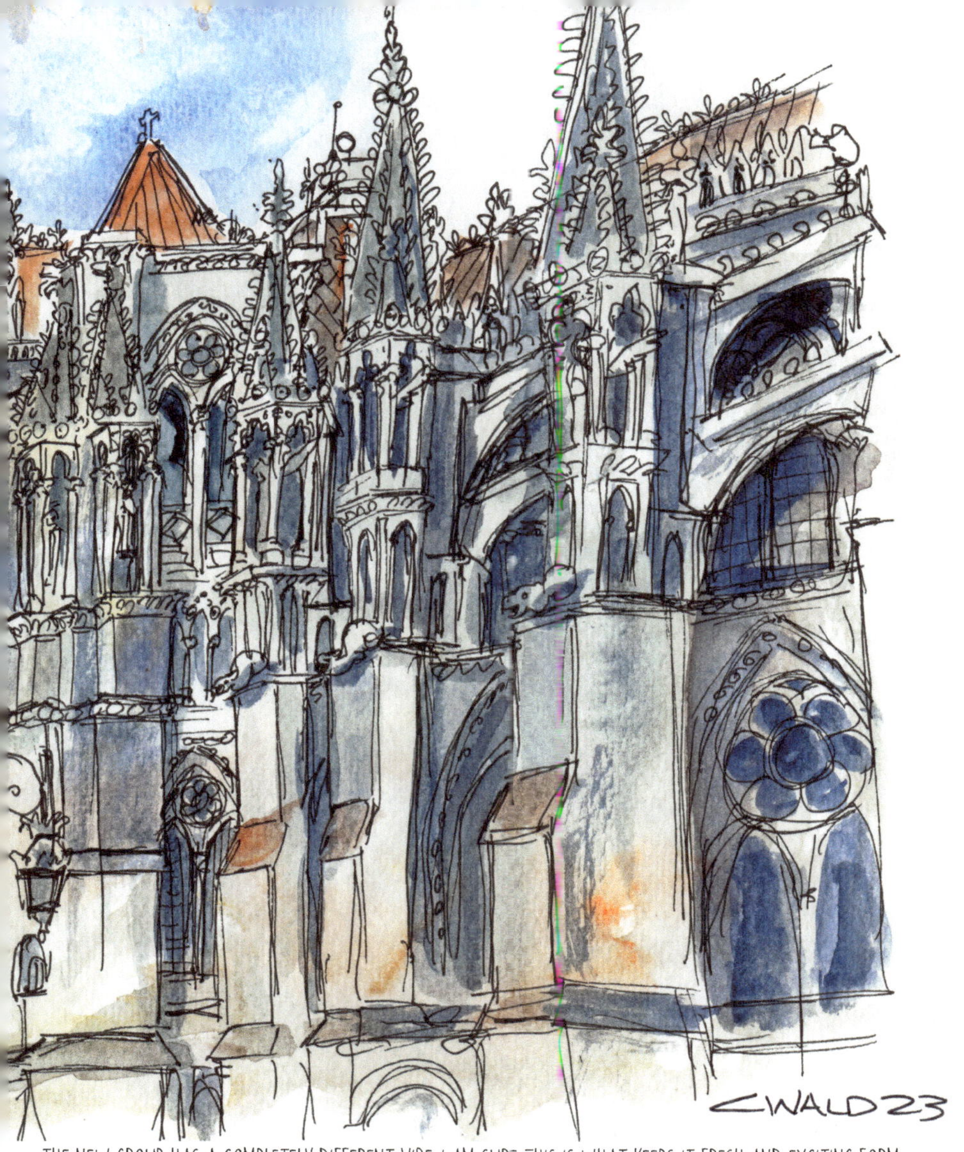

THE NEW GROUP HAS A COMPLETELY DIFFERENT VIBE. I AM SURE THIS IS WHAT KEEPS IT FRESH AND EXCITING FORM ZIGGY AND BEULAH. EVERY GROUP HAS A UNIQUE DYNAMIC. THERE ARE SOME GAMERS IN THE GROUP WHICH IS CLOSE TO MY HEART. MANY OF THE SECOND GROUP WERE YOUNGER AND THERE WERE MORE ARTISTS FROM CANADA AND AUSTRALIA. ONCE AGAIN. THERE WAS A WELCOME DINNER OF BOEUF BOURGUIGNON. DUSTY WELCOMED THE NEWCOMERS BY LOUNGING ON THE TABLE WHILE PEOPLE ATE. NO ONE MADE HIM MOVE.

I ALSO MET MY NEW HOUSE NEIGHBOR. JENNIFER. WHO TOOK ROXY'S ROOM. WE SHARE A LITTLE ENTRYWAY TO OUR ROOMS EVEN THOUGH THEY ARE PRIVATE. JONATHAN OFFERED MANY THE OPPORTUNITY TO LOSE TO HIM AT CHESS.

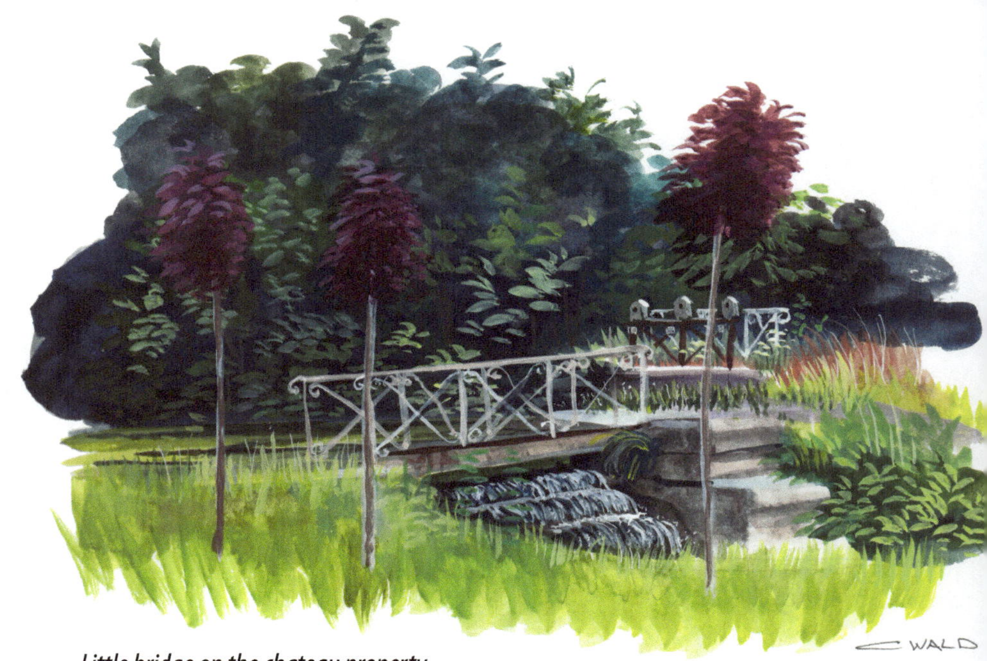

Little bridge on the chateau property.

WE WENT SHOPPING TODAY AND I DROVE THIS TIME. AS USUAL, DRIVING IS ALWAYS AN ADVENTURE.

I FOUND A GOOD DEAL ON CLEARANCE ARCHES PAPER. I HAD NOT BEEN THRILLED WITH THE WATERCOLOR PAPER I PURCHASED AT THE LAST VISIT.

I AM STILL NOT USED TO HAVING A DIESEL CAR. I FOUND OUT THAT THERE ARE TWO NOZZLE SIZES AND OF COURSE I PAID FOR THE WRONG ONE FIRST. MOST GAS STATIONS ARE COMPLETELY SELF-SERVE. FORTUNATELY, I WAS NOT CHARGED FOR MY BUMBLING.

I DID NOT REALIZE HOW EXHAUSTED I WAS FROM EVERYTHING AND I WENT TO BED AT 10PM.
NO SKETCHING TODAY.

DAY 17

I STARTED OUT THE DAY DOING LAUNDRY AND FINISHED MY SALES TAX FILING THAT HUNG OVER MY HEAD FOR THE FIRST TWO WEEKS. I WAS FREE AT LAST!

AFTER DINNER, ZIGGY TALKED ABOUT THE HISTORY OF THE CHATEAU.

THE CHATEAU ITSELF IS A HUNTING CASTLE. THE RESIDENCE CHATEAU D'ORQUEVAUX OR CHATEAU D'VANGEUL WAS BUILT NEXT TO THE STABLES IN THE 1700S. SADLY, IT WAS DEMOLISHED IN 2002.

You can still see the ice house.

Once the home of Denis Diderot, french philosopher, art critic, and writer, Chateau d'Orquevaux was built in the early 1700s for his uncle Charles Denis du Vandeul. His family owned the property until the death of Diderot's last direct descendant, Albert Vasndeul, who died in 1911 in Paris. Notably, he had the church moved do he could build his mistress a castle overlooking the village.

The Saint Exupéry family bought the chateau in 1918 and kept it until 1987 except when the Nazi's used the chateau as a base of operations during World War II. When the Nazi's fled, they took all the furniture with them.

Antoine de Saint Exupéry, author of **The Little Prince**, an his family visited often.

A bunch of Diderot's writings were discovered in the chateau and published in 1951.

Ziggy inherited the chateau from his father in 2016 and partnered with Beulah to start the artist residency.

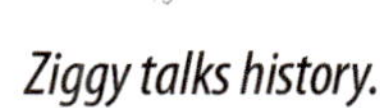

Ziggy talks history.

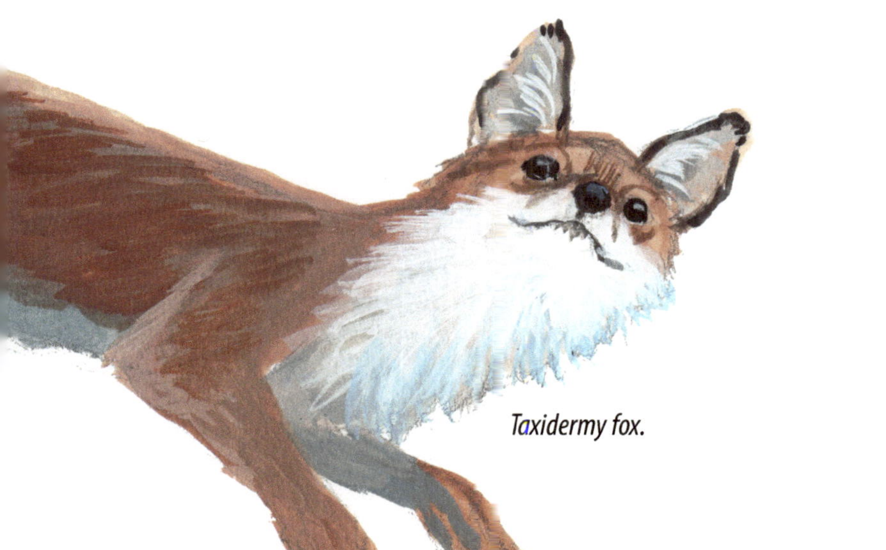

Taxidermy fox.

DAY 18

THE BEST LAID PLANS

I HAD INVITED EVERYONE TO JOIN ME TO SKETCH THE CASTLE. ONLY A FEW JOINED ME AND WE WERE STOPPED BY STEADY RAIN. FORTUNATELY, LIBIA WAS ABLE TO SPEAK ENOUGH FRENCH WITH ERIC, THE GROUNDS KEEPER, TO ARRANGE FOR US TO NOT ONLY SKETCH THERE, BUT ON THE GROUNDS THE FOLLOWING SUNDAY.

THE REST OF THE DAY, I WORKED IN THE STUDIO.

THERE ARE A BUNCH OF GAMERS IN THIS GROUP! WE PLAYED MILLE BORNES AND YAHTZEE UNTIL LATE. I ALSO LOOKED UP A GAME STORE IN NANCY, WHERE WE PLAN TO TAKE A ROAD TRIP TOMORROW.

DAY 19

A DAY IN NANCY

GREG, LEIGH, AND I DROVE TO THE LOVELY CITY OF NANCY. IT IS FAMOUS FOR ITS ART NOUVEAU ARCHITECTURE. I HAD MADE SURE TO LOOK UP WHERE TO PARK BEFORE WE LEFT SO I COULD NAVIGATE THERE. THE DRIVE WAS FUN AS GREG AND LEIGH DISCUSSED PICK-UP LINES IN FRENCH, MANY INCORPORATING THE WORD DERRIÈRE.

WE HAD LUNCH AT A RESTAURANT BY THE TOWN SQUARE WITH A COMIC BOOK THEMED DECOR. I HAD FISH AND CHIPS, GOOD BUT I REGRETTED NOT GETTING THE MUSSELS.

I THEN FOUND THE GAME STORE WHILE GREG AND LEIGH EXPLORED. THEY HAD A REALLY GOOD SELECTION AND THE PROPRIETORS OF GAME STORES LOOK THE SAME ALL OVER THE WORLD. I GOT **SUSHI GO** AND **SPLENDOR**. THEY ARE BOTH FAIRLY EASY AND I KNEW THE RULES WELL ENOUGH SINCE THESE EDITIONS WERE IN FRENCH.

AFTER I DROPPED THE GAMES IN THE CAR, I SCOUTED A GOOD PLACE TO SKETCH. IT WAS SUCH A HARD DECISION BUT I DECIDED ON THE FOUNTAIN DEPICTING NEPTUNE. IT WAS

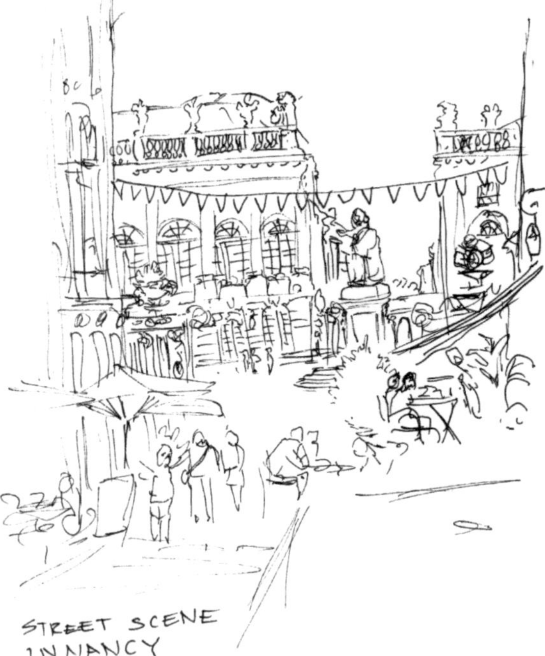

STREET SCENE
IN NANCY

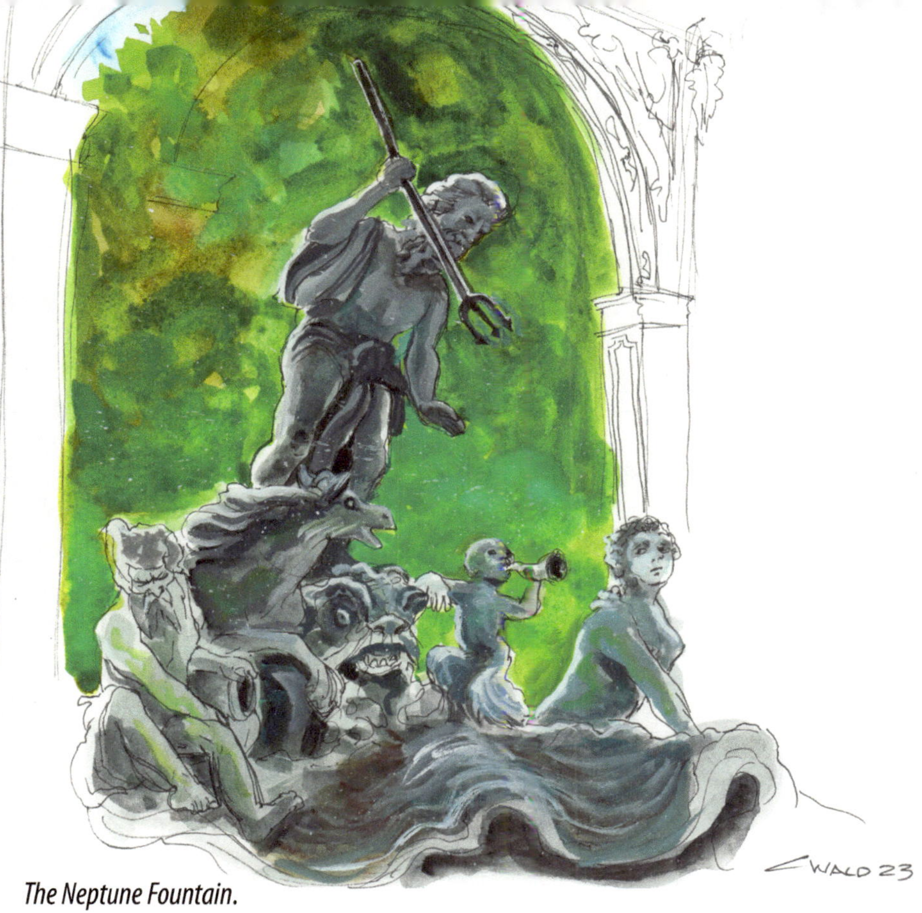

The Neptune Fountain.

DESIGNED IN ROCOCO-STYLE BY BARTHELEMY GUIBAL AND HAD A STRANGELY MIDDLE-AGED LOOKING CHERUB. THE PEOPLE WATCHING WAS SUPERB AS PEOPLE TRIED TO GET THEIR CHILDREN AND PETS TO COOPERATE AS THEY TOOK PHOTOS IN FRONT OF THE FOUNTAIN. AFTER A DAY OF RAIN, THE WEATHER WAS BEAUTIFUL FOR SKETCHING.

IT WAS A SATURDAY SO THERE WAS A STREAM OF WEDDING PARTIES THAT CAME TO THE BALCONY OF THE TOWN HALL FACING THE SQUARE. CHEERED BY THEIR GUESTS. IT SEEMED TO HAPPEN EACH HOUR.

WE ATTEMPTED TO VISIT A CASTLE BUT IT WAS CLOSED AND HEADED BACK TO THE CHATEAU AS USUAL TO BE BACK BY DINNER. THE PARKING GARAGE WAS COMICALLY TIGHT SO IT TOOK A BIT OF MANEUVERING, SHOUTING, AND PRAYING TO GET OUT OF OUR PARKING SPACE. PAYING FOR THE PARKING WAS ALSO A CHALLENGE.

I DID NOT REALIZE HOW EXHAUSTED I WAS BUT I WAS ASLEEP BY 9PM.

DAY 20

♜ STORMING THE CASTLE ♜

A MUCH LARGER GROUP OF US STROLLED UP THE HILL TO CASTEL D'ORQUEVAUX!

ERIC WAS WAITING FOR US AS HOPED. WE STREAMED IN THROUGH THE GATES. I INSTANTLY FELL IN LOVE WITH THE SOLARIUM AT THE BACK. THERE WERE SO MANY INTERESTING TOUCHES THAT ADDED TO ITS FANTASY LAND FEEL FROM THE FAKE CAVE TO THE CONCRETE RAILINGS MOLDED INTO THE SHAPE OF BRANCHES.

THERE WAS ALSO A GARDEN. IT LOOKED LIKE IT WAS TORN FROM THE PAGES OF A STORYBOOK.
I DECIDED TO JUST DO AN INK SKETCH OF THE BACK OF THE CASTLE SO I COULD DRAW THE SOLARIUM. SINCE I HAD PAINTED IT TWICE BEFORE FROM DIFFERENT VANTAGE POINTS. I WANTED A COMPLETELY DIFFERENT FEEL TO THE SKETCH.

AS WAS MENTIONED DURING THE HISTORY OF THE CHATEAU. THE CHURCH WAS MOVED TO BUILD THE CASTLE FOR VASNDEUL'S MISTRESS. ITS CONSTRUCTION IS DEFINITELY MORE FAIRYTALE THAN FORTIFICATION.

FIRE PIT

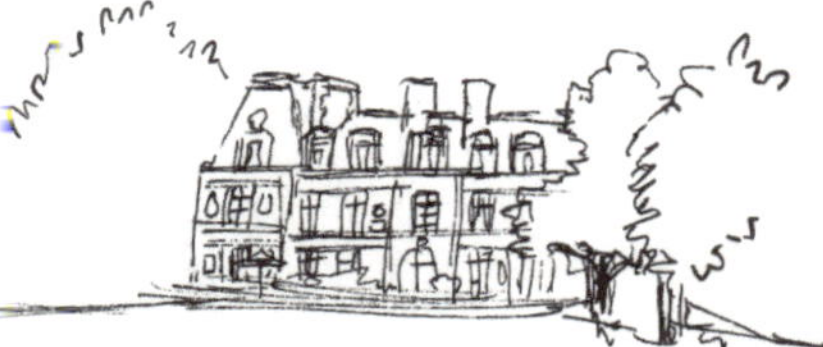

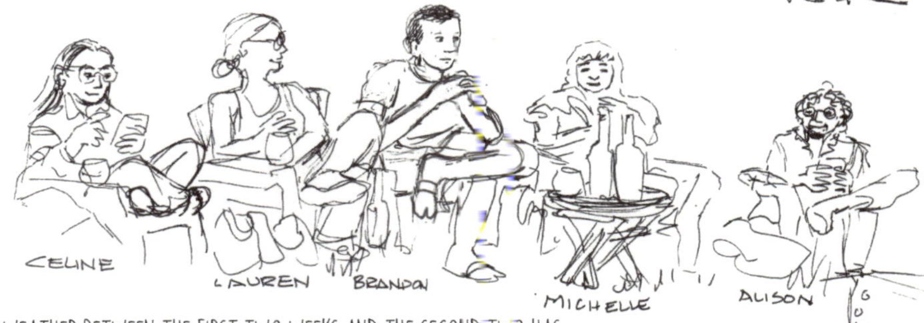

THE WEATHER BETWEEN THE FIRST TWO WEEKS AND THE SECOND TWO HAS BEEN COMPLETELY DIFFERENT. THERE WERE PLANS SEVERAL DAYS DURING THE FIRST HALF TO HAVE A FIRE PIT ONE EVENING BUT IT WAS TOO HOT AND DRY WITH A REAL DANGER OF A FOREST FIRE.

IT WAS MUCH COOLER AND WE HAD SOME RAIN SO WE WERE FINALLY ABLE TO SIT AROUND A FIRE. WE WROTE DOWN SOMETHING WE WANTED TO LET GO OF IN OUR LIFE AND BURNED IT IN THE FIRE. THERE WAS ALSO SINGING. SOME OF THIS SECOND GROUP OF ARTISTS HAD VERY GOOD VOICES AND MIKE BROUGHT HIS GUITAR. WE WERE SUPPOSED TO FILL IN A REFRAIN THAT HE PLAYED IN BLUES FASHION AS HIS WIFE CHRISTINE WORKED THE CROWD. THEY HAD SUCH GREAT ENERGY.

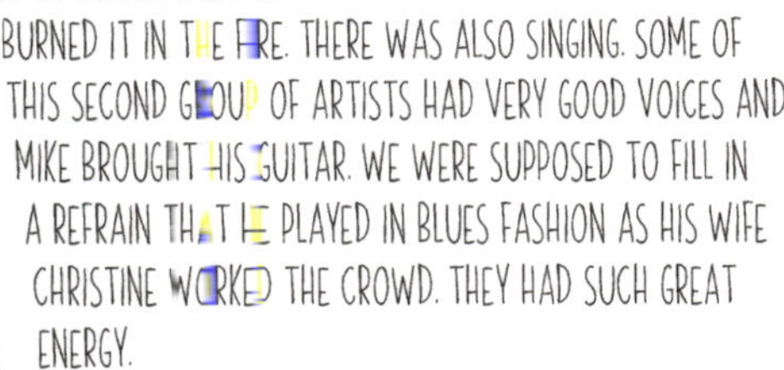

THE PARTY WENT WAY INTO THE NIGHT. BUT I WENT TO BED. THE GRASS ONLY CAUGHT FIRE ONCE!

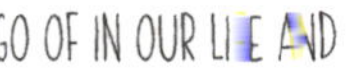

The fire pit at last.

DAY 21

EACH TWO-WEEK RESIDENCY. THEY HAVE LIFE DRAWING. I MISSED THE FIRST SESSION BECAUSE WE VISITED DIJON. I WAS ABLE TO GO TO THIS SESSION. I LIKE LIFE DRAWING ALTHOUGH I REALLY PREFER SKETCHING PEOPLE IN COSTUME RATHER THAN NUDE. I USED TO GO TO REGULAR DR SKETCHY'S SESSIONS WHEN THEY HAD THEM IN COVINGTON, KENTUCKY. THEY HAD MODELS DRESSED ACCORDING TO A THEME ALTHOUGH THY GREW OUT OF BURLESQUE PERFORMANCE. I GUESS IT PROBABLY HAS TO DO WITH MY LOVE OF NARRATIVE STORYTELLING. THIS WAS A GOOD OPPORTUNITY TO SKETCH WITH OUR WHOLE GROUP OF CREATIVES.

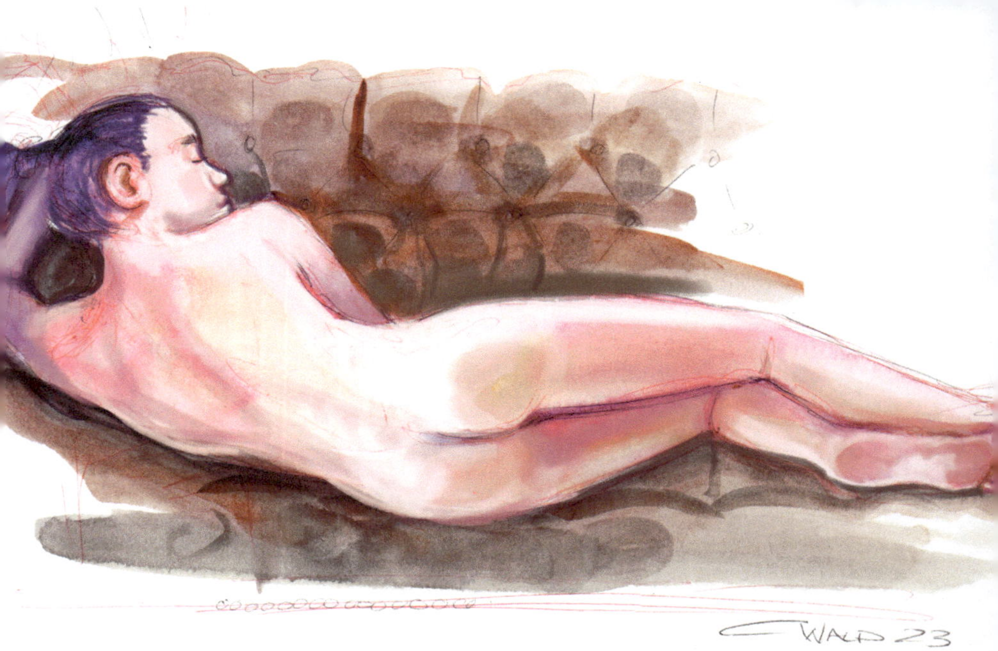

EVEN SOME OF THE WRITERS JOINED IN. THE MODEL COMES OVER WITH A DANISH PHOTOGRAPHER EVERY COUPLE OF WEEKS AND THEY STAY FOR DINNER AND CONVERSATION.

THE PHOTOGRAPHER HAS TAKEN PHOTOS ALL OVER THE GROUNDS AND OCCASIONALLY OF SOME OF THE RESIDENTS. HE IS DEFINITELY A CHARACTER. I ACTUALLY WOULD LOVE TO SEE A LIFE DRAWING SETUP WHERE THE MODELS DRESS IN OUTFITS USING THE COSTUME ROOM.

THE DAY CONCLUDED WITH SOME GAMES STARTING WITH SUSHI GO AND SPLENDOR. THE GROUP EVENTUALLY RETIRED TO THE BASEMENT FOR SINGING, DANCING, AND CARDS.

DAY 22

IT WAS ANOTHER RAINY DAY. EVERYONE GATHERED IN THE SALON AFTER DINNER TO WORK TOGETHER RATHER THAN TALKING AND GENERALLY HANGING AROUND TALKING OUTSIDE LIKE USUAL.

THERE WAS A REALLY NICE VIBE AS EVERYONE SKETCHED, TALKED, AND WROTE.

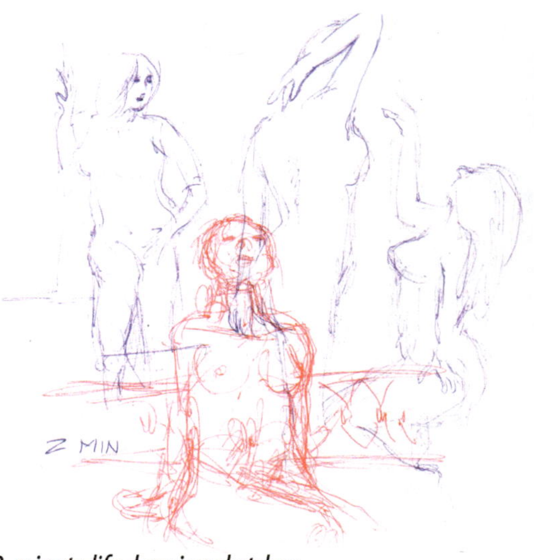

2-minute life drawing sketches.

SEVERAL PEOPLE WERE WRITING POETRY
AND DISCUSSING THE METER AND LANGUAGE
THEY WERE USING. IMPROMPTU READINGS
BROKE OUT.

THE NIGHT WAS MISTY AND GORGEOUS DUE
TO THE RAIN. THE LIGHT WAS ETHEREAL.
ZIGGY GOT A FEW PHOTOS OF THE CHATEAU
AND I COULD NOT RESIST DOING A LITTLE
GOUACHE PAINTING OF IT.

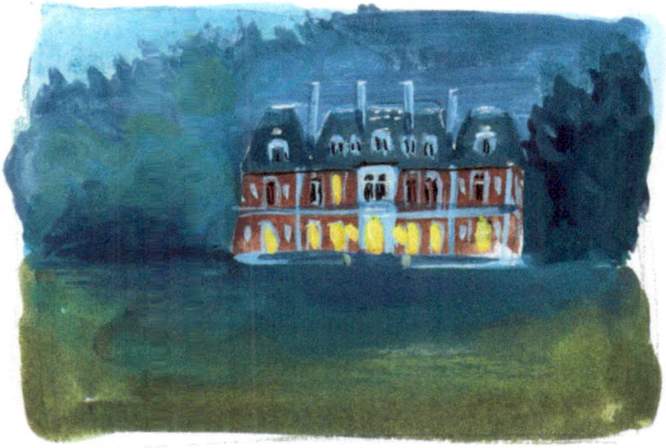

MISTY CHATEAU, 7.25.23

LIBIA STARTED DOING PRIVATE TAROT READINGS WHICH WENT ON FOR A FEW DAYS AS
THE WORD GOT OUT AND MORE PEOPLE REQUESTED THEM.

DAY 23

I SPENT THE MORNING WORKING ON THE TRAVELOGUE. I SPENT A QUITE A WHILE TINKERING WITH THE INSIDE
COVER DESIGN. BEULAH WAS DOING HER ART BUSINESS TALK THAT MORNING AND I ALTHOUGH I DID NOT ATTEND
THE WHOLE DISCUSSION, I CAME DOWN TO WATCH RACHEL'S TALK ABOUT PUBLISHING. SHE WRITE AND LAYS OUT

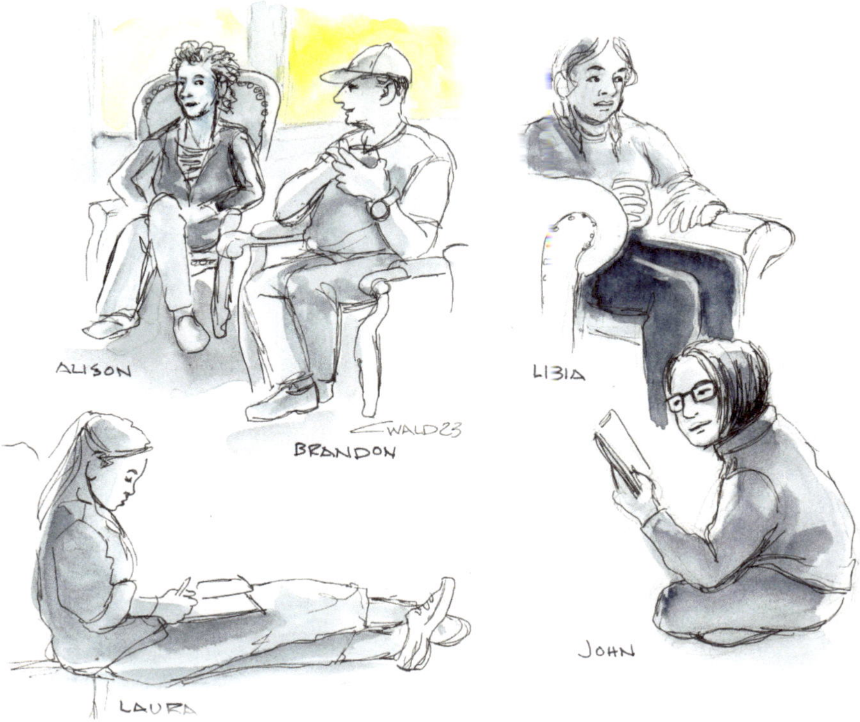

ALISON

GWALD23
BRANDON

LIBIA

JOHN

LAURA

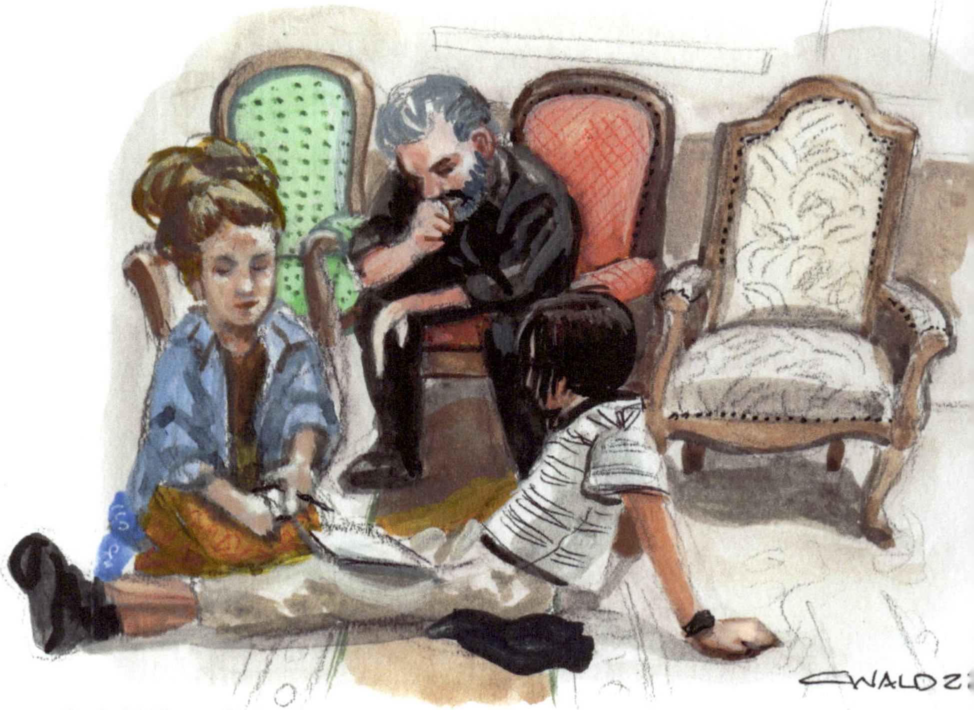

Rachel, Mike, and John discuss a stanza.

BOOKS. MOSTLY POETRY. I HAVE ILLUSTRATED SO MANY BOOKS AND AM JUST NOW LEARNING TO LAY THEM OUT. INCLUDING THIS ONE.

SINCE THE WEATHER WAS SO COMFORTABLE. I TOOK THE OPPORTUNITY TO SKETCH THE GATEHOUSE. I HAD MY EYE ON IT FOR A WHILE AND TIME IS RUNNING OUT BEFORE I LEAVE. SADLY. THIS MEANT I WOULD MISS A SHOWING OF MOVIE SHORTS WRITTEN BY MELISSA AND ALISON IN THE SALON.

I FOUND A PERFECT SPOT AND WAS ONLY RAINED ON A LITTLE. IT FELT REMOTE AND ONLY AN OCCASIONAL CAR PASSED BY. THE SMELL OF THE WET GRASS. THE SOUNDS OF BIRDS. THE LIGHT BREEZE AND CONSTANTLY CHANGING LIGHT FROM THE RAPIDLY MOVING CLOUDS WERE EVERYTHING SKETCHING ON LOCATION SHOULD BE.

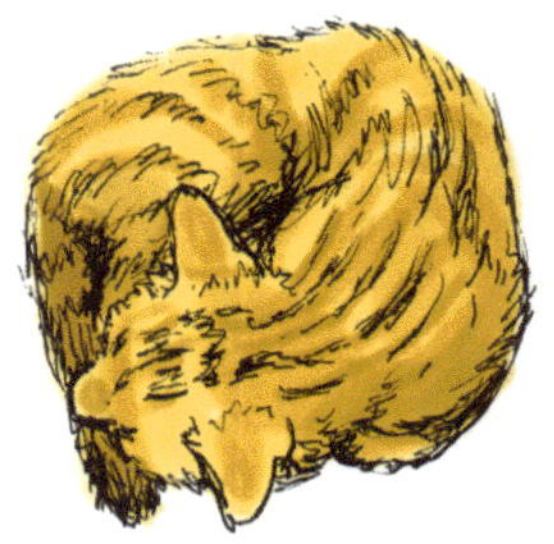

WE SPENT A LOW KEY EVENING IN THE SALON PLAYING CARDS WITH DUSTY CURLED UP NEXT TO ME. I LOST THE GAME SO HE WAS NOT GIVING ANY CAT GOOD LUCK. IT WAS HARD TO MOVE A SLEEPING CAT TO GO TO BED.

Dusty in sleep mode.

DAY 24

EVERY MORNING, I WAKE UP TO THE SOUND OF COWS MOOING. SOMETIMES IT IS CONVERSATIONAL. OTHER TIMES IT IS IN DISTRESS. THERE WAS ONE DAY THAT ONE OF THE COWS WAS DISTRAUGHT. SHE MOOED ALL DAY. I SUSPECT SOMEONE, MAYBE A CALF, WAS TAKEN FROM THE HERD.

I COULD SEE THEM FROM MY WINDOW BUT WAS NOT TOTALLY SURE HOW TO GET TO THEM IN ORDER TO SKETCH THEM. I ASKED AROUND AND FOUND OUT THEY MOVED TO SEVERAL DIFFERENT FIELDS. I WALKED DOWN THE ROAD WHERE I HAD SKETCHED THE GATEHOUSE THE DAY BEFORE AND FOUND A BIG HERD! THE FIELD HAD BEEN EMPTY THE DAY BEFORE. IT WAS FUN TO WATCH AND PHOTOGRAPH THEM.

AT ONE POINT, A COW CLOSE TO ME AND THE FENCE STARTED TO MOO WITH EXCITEMENT! I TURNED TO SEE A

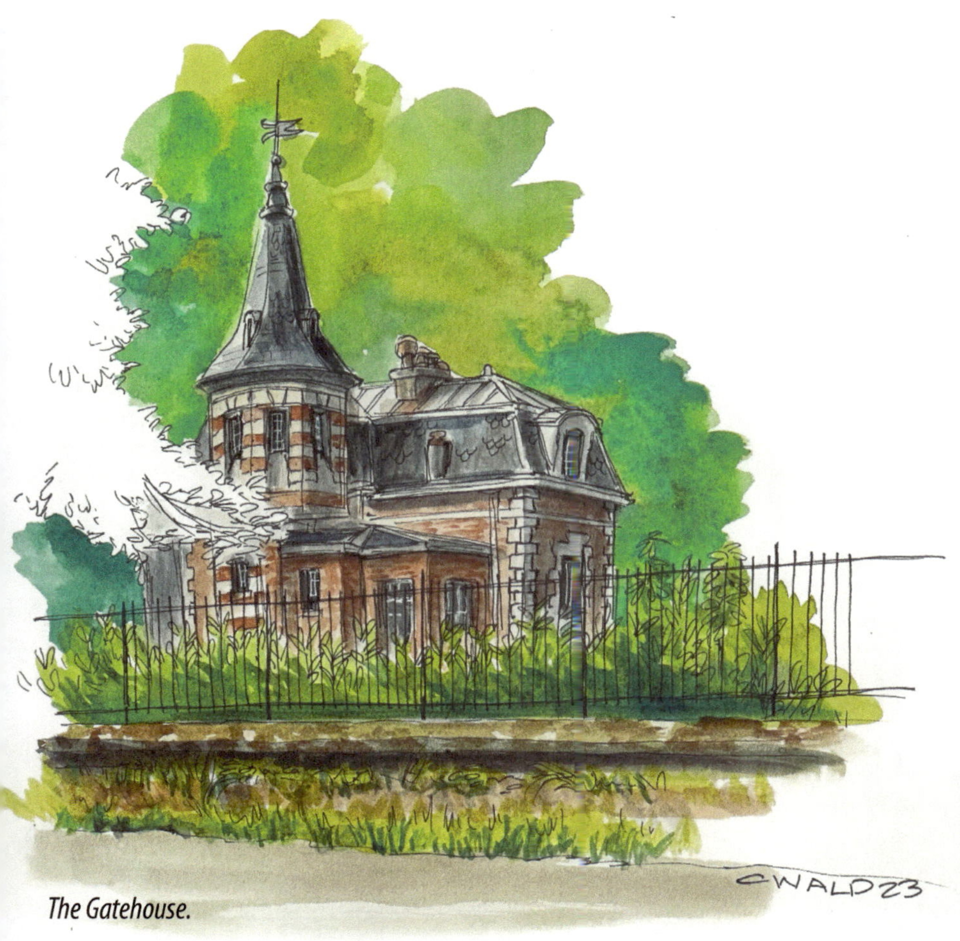

The Gatehouse.

TRACTOR COMING DOWN THE ROAD WITH A HUGE HAY BALE ATTACHED. THE GATE OPENED AND THE TRACTOR DROVE IN THE PADDOCK TOWARDS THE FEEDER. MORE COWS MOOED AND AMBLED TO THE TRACTOR WITH ALACRITY. IT WAS QUITE THE PAGEANT!

I WENT BACK TO MY STUDIO AND FINALLY PAINTED MY COWS IN GOUACHE. THE TRACTOR WAS DIFFERENT THAN ANY I HAD SEEN BEFORE AND WAS A FRENCH BRAND CALLED MANITOU. THE DESIGN WAS REFRESHING AND MODERN. THE MANUFACTURER ALSO MAKES OTHER VEHICLES LIKE FORKLIFTS AND BACKHOES.

DURING THE FIRST HALF OF THE RESIDENCY, I HAD NOT SEEN THE ART STUDIOS IN THE STABLES UNTIL THE OPEN STUDIOS. I DECIDED TO VISIT THE STABLES AND SEE THEM AND THE ARTISTS WORKING THERE BEFORE OUR FINAL PRESENTATION.

I WAS SO GLAD I DID. IT WAS INTERESTING TO SEE THE WORKSPACES BUZZING WITH ACTIVITY LIKE WELDING, SCULPTING, PAINTING, COLLAGE, AND MORE. I OFTEN GET SO FOCUSED ON WHAT I AM WORKING ON THAT I FORGET TO LOOK UP AND SEE THE WORLD AROUND.

Happy cows.

WE ALSO SAW A BAT HANGING IN THE ENTRANCE TO LEIGH'S STUDIO THAT WE NEVER DETERMINED IF IT WAS ALIVE. BATS ARE LIVING ON THE UNFINISHED SECOND FLOOR*

*NOTE: THE UPSTAIRS OF THE STABLES HAVE BEEN REFINISHED SINCE I LEFT.

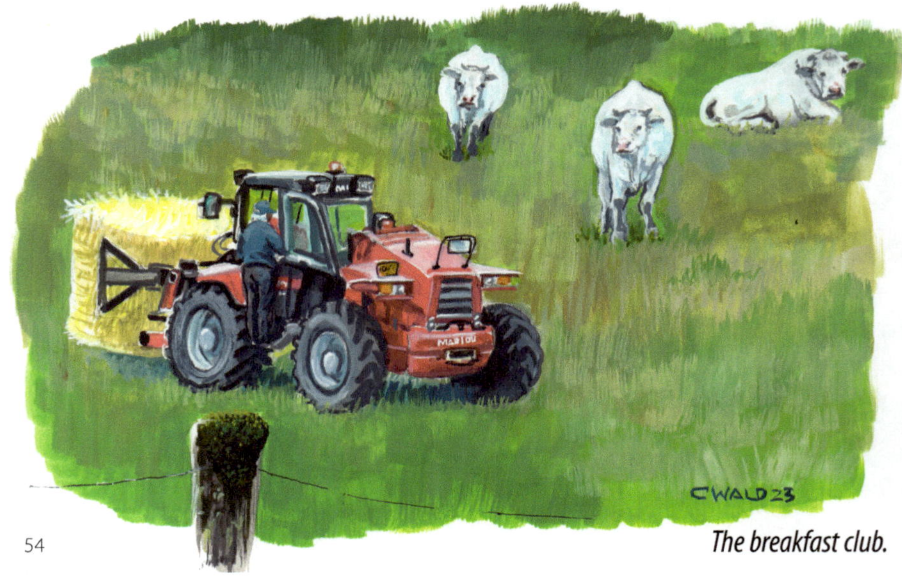

The breakfast club.

IT WAS ANOTHER EARLY NIGHT; I WAS EXHAUSTED.

DAY 25

IT WAS A DAY OF PREPARATION FOR OPEN STUDIO AND THE LITERATURE SALON.

THERE WERE SO MANY MOVING READINGS THIS TIME. I GAVE SEVERAL QUOTES FROM JULIA CHILD, MY HERO. I DO NOT HAVE THE WORDS TO ACCURATELY DESCRIBE THESE MEETINGS BUT I THINK THEY INVOKE THE CREATIVE SPIRIT OF THE RESIDENCY PROGRAM. I WAS FORTUNATE TO BE INVOLVED IN TWO OF THEM. BEFORE THE RESIDENCY, I NEVER REALLY CAME INTO CONTACT WITH POETS EXCEPT FOR THOSE WHO WRITE THEM FOR CHILDREN'S LITERATURE AND READINGS AT THE ART ACADEMY. I LEFT WITH A RESPECT FOR THEM AND APPRECIATION OF THEIR WORK.

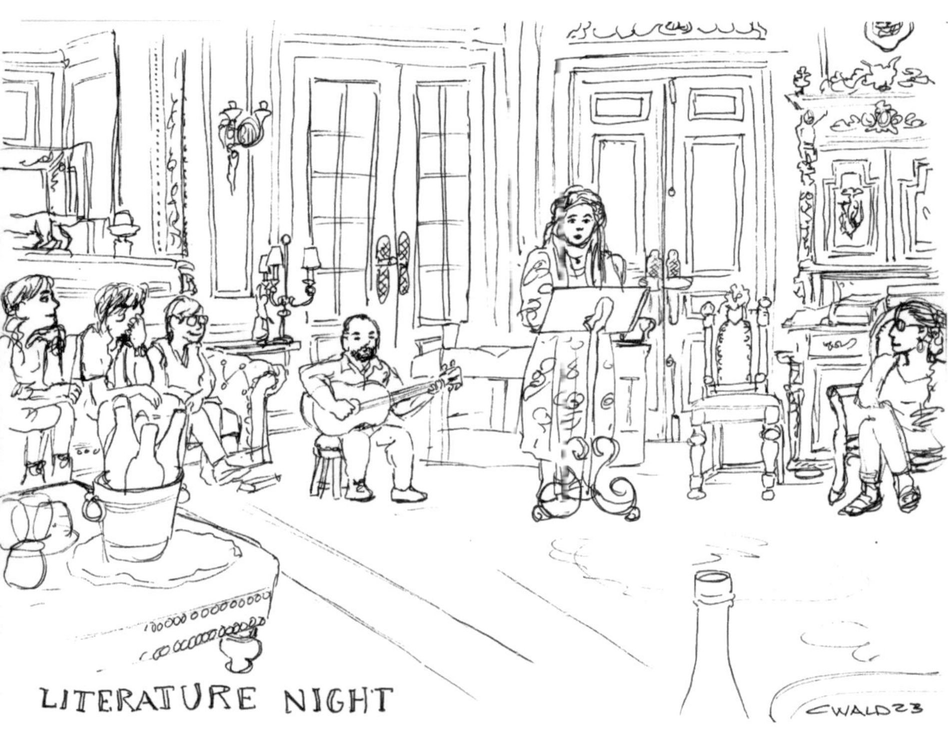

THE REST OF THE DAY WAS CRUNCH TIME. I FINISHED A SKETCH OF THE CANAL AT THE GATE TO THE CHATEAU GROUNDS, CLEANED MY STUDIO, AND FINISHED MY TRAVELOGUE PRESENTATION, FRANTICALLY LAYING OUT A FEW PAGES. I WAS UP TILL 2 OR 3 AM. THERE WERE A FEW OF US TIPTOEING AROUND.

ALTHOUGH THERE IS NO PRESSURE TO PRODUCE DURING THE RESIDENCY, IT IS FASCINATING TO SEE, HEAR, WATCH, AND READ THE WORKS OF EVERYONE. THEY ARE AN ATTRACTIVE BYPRODUCT OF THE EXPERIENCE. THESES WORKS ARE JUST SEEDS THAT WILL FUEL FUTURE ARTISTIC ENDEAVORS.

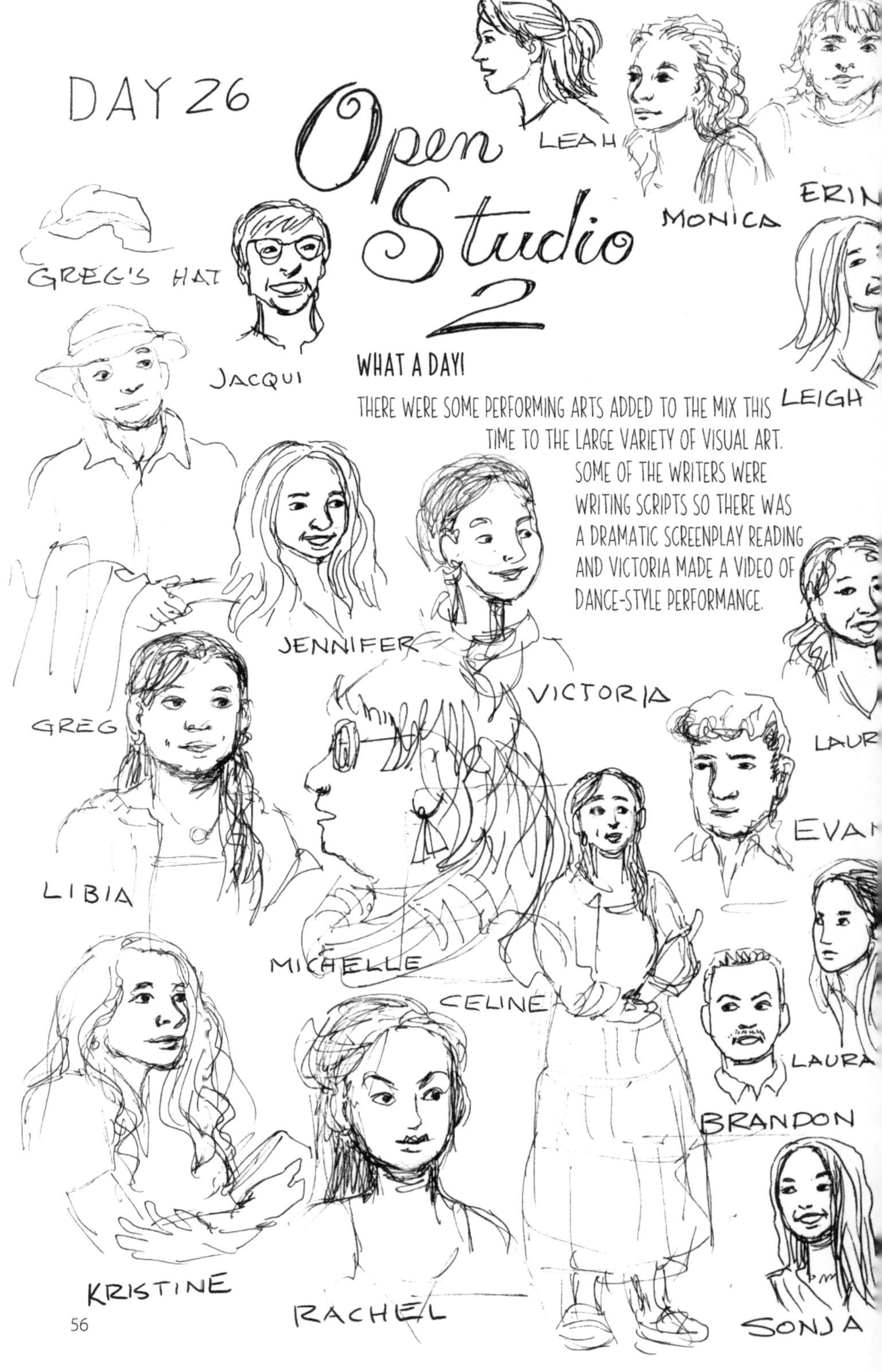

DAY 26
Open Studio 2
GREG'S HAT
JACQUI
LEAH
MONICA
ERIN
LEIGH
WHAT A DAY!
THERE WERE SOME PERFORMING ARTS ADDED TO THE MIX THIS
TIME TO THE LARGE VARIETY OF VISUAL ART.
SOME OF THE WRITERS WERE
WRITING SCRIPTS SO THERE WAS
A DRAMATIC SCREENPLAY READING
AND VICTORIA MADE A VIDEO OF
DANCE-STYLE PERFORMANCE.
JENNIFER
VICTORIA
GREG
LIBIA
MICHELLE
CELINE
LAUR
EVAN
KRISTINE
RACHEL
BRANDON
LAURA
SONJA
56

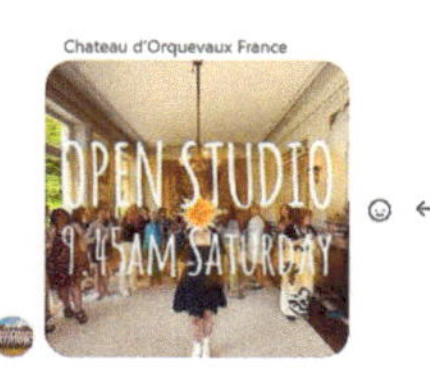

Chateau d'Orquevaux France

OPEN STUDIO

Starting at 9.45am in dining room, straight from Breakfast
The Days Events
~
Open Studio Day will begin in the dining Salon with a few words from our Residency Director Beulah,
~
We begin Open Studio visits in the Salon with our writers/film makers, Kristina, Monica, Alison
~
Heading into Esther's Bath for Rachel & Laura's Atelier Presentation.
~
We will make our way to the Chateau Studio floor beginning in Atelier #7, Greg's making our way down the hallway and ending in Atelier #1, Jonathan, for the final presentation of the morning before making our way downstairs straight to the steps for our Residency Steps photoghraph
~
LUNCH, BREAK TIME & RELAX
♥ 🧡

Chateau d'Orquevaux France

3.30pm Starting in the Dining Salon for 🥖 & 🍷 & 🧀
Before we head down to Stables Studios 🏠 around 4pm
~
We start then start at Stables Studios
~
Atelier #8,Victoria's Atelier presentation of work followed by Atelier #7, Lauren and following the Stables Studios circle around to end in Atelier #1, Leah's Atelier
~
We head back upstairs to conclude the day with.....DINNER
~
"I don't think about art when I'm working. I try to think about life." Jean-Michel Basquiat
👍 ❤ 3

Beulah's schedule of the open studio in Instagram.

FORTUNATELY, THE OPEN STUDIO IS NOT THE LAST DAY OF THE RESIDENCY BECAUSE IT IS AN INTENSE DAY. THE WINE IS FLOWING TO DIFFUSE FRAYED NERVES. AFTERWARD, EVERYONE IS SO RELAXED AS THE PRESSURE OF EXPLAINING ONE'S WORK TO THE WHOLE GROUP IS OVER!

NOT ONLY WAS THERE A DANCE PARTY, IT WAS A KARAOKE DANCE PARTY IN COSTUME. THE KARAOKE MACHINE HAD ISSUES CONNECTING TO THE PROJECTOR SO WE USED MY LAPTOP AND I INADVERTENTLY BECAME A DJ FOR THE EVENING. I AM NOT A HUGE FAN OF DANCING OR SINGING SO IT WAS A PERFECT WAY TO JOIN THE FESTIVITIES. (I ALSO DID NOT WANT MY COMPUTER KNOCKED TO THE FLOOR. THERE IS A LOT OF WORK STORED THERE.)

THE PARTY WAS STILL GOING STRONG AT 2AM WHEN I COULD NO LONGER KEEP MY EYES OPEN AND HEADED UP TO BED.

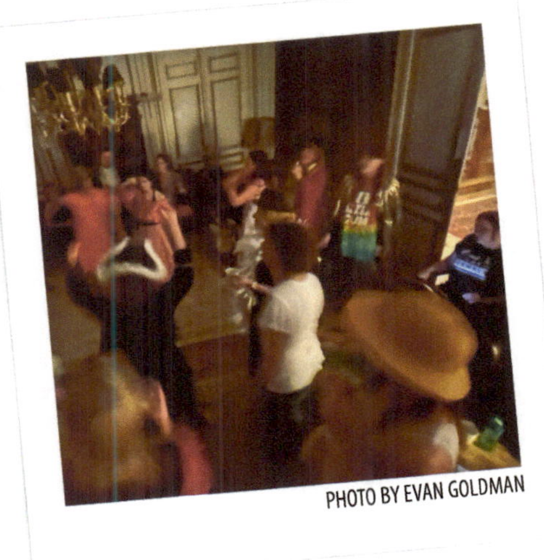

PHOTO BY EVAN GOLDMAN

Karaoke dance party in costume.

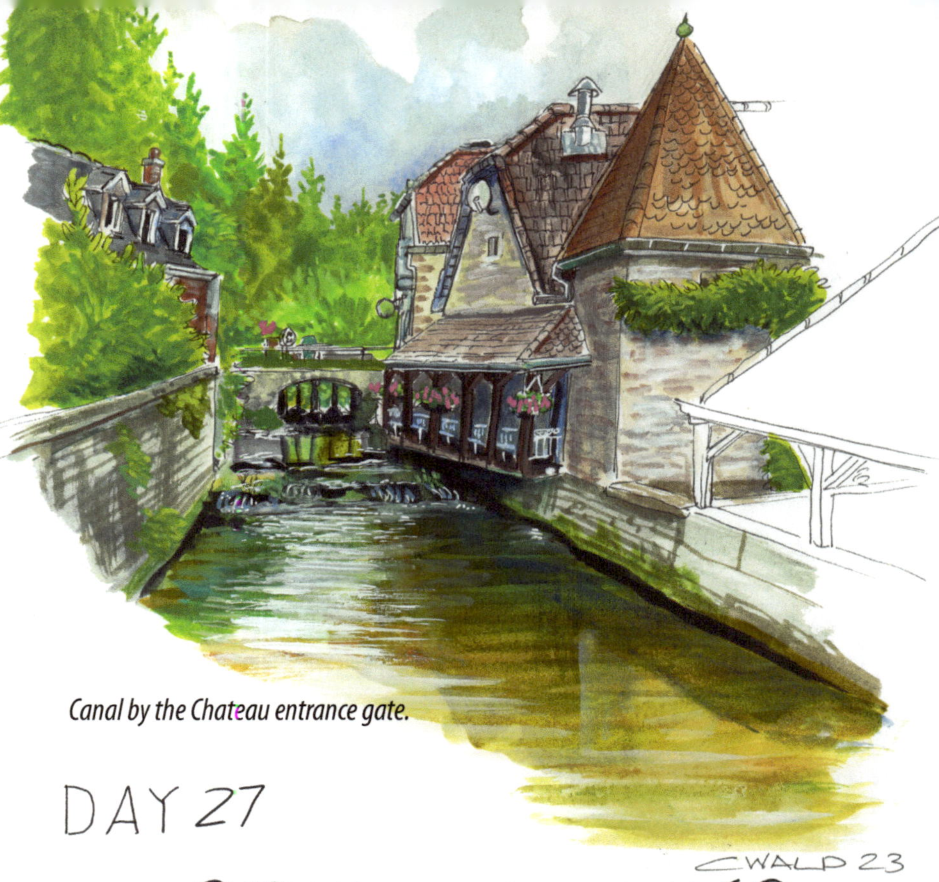

Canal by the Chateau entrance gate.

DAY 27

CWALD 23

☹ THE LAST DAY ☹

WE DECIDED TO DO ONE LAST CAR ADVENTURE AND TOOK A SHORT TRIP TO JOINVILLE. A TOWN CLOSE TO THE CHATEAU THAT HAS ITS OWN CHATEAU AND GARDENS. LEIGH. GREG. VICTORIA. AND I SET OFF TO EXPLORE

THE TOWN WAS UNEXPECTEDLY BUSTLING FOR A SUNDAY. WE STOPPED BY A BAKERY AND THEN WALKED AROUND. EVENTUALLY COMING UPON A CHURCH IN THE MIDDLE OF RENOVATIONS. THERE WERE DISPLAYS EXPLAINING THE LOCAL HISTORY AND SOMEONE WAS PLAYING MUSIC ON THE ORGAN THE WHOLE TIME. OUR PLAN TO VISIT THE CHATEAU AND GARDENS WAS QUASHED WHEN WE FOUND OUT THEY CLOSED FROM 12 UNTIL 2PM. AND WE RETURNED BEFORE LUNCH.

YESTERDAY. ZIGGY SUGGESTED I PAINT ERIC'S HOUSE AT THE ENTRANCE OF THE CHATEAU SINCE HE SO KINDLY LET US SKETCH ON THE CASTLE GROUNDS. IT WAS THE PERFECT WAY TO SPEND THE LAST DAY! MANY OF THE OTHERS WENT FOR A LAST VISIT TO THE SUNFLOWER FIELD BY THE CASTLE ON THE HILL. AS I SKETCHED. SOME TOURISTS STOPPED BY THE CHATEAU AND LOOKED AROUND. A COMMON OCCURRENCE APPARENTLY. MORE PEOPLE STOPPED BY TO CHAT THAN USUAL.

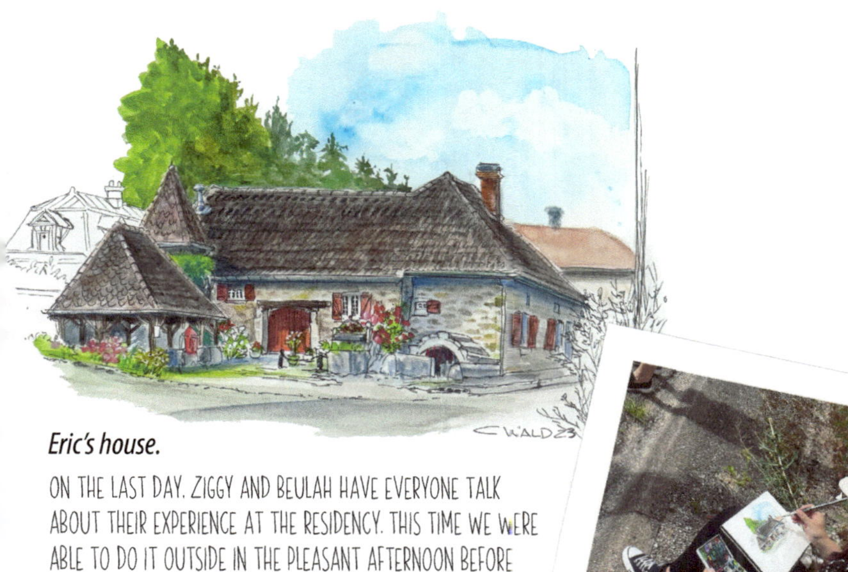

Eric's house.

ON THE LAST DAY. ZIGGY AND BEULAH HAVE EVERYONE TALK ABOUT THEIR EXPERIENCE AT THE RESIDENCY. THIS TIME WE WERE ABLE TO DO IT OUTSIDE IN THE PLEASANT AFTERNOON BEFORE DINNER.

IT WAS AN EMOTIONAL FOR EVERYONE. ESPECIALLY FOR KAT. EVAN. GREG AND ME WHO HAD BEEN THERE FOR A MONTH. THERE IS SOMETHING THAT HAPPENS WHEN YOU ARE WITH A GROUP OF PEOPLE EVERYDAY. SHARING MEALS AND CONVERSATION. OUTSIDE OF THE BLARE OF CONSTANT MEDIA BOMBARDMENT. MEANINGFUL ATTACHMENTS ARE FORMED AND IT HAS A LASTING IMPACT ON EVERYONE.

PHOTO BY LAURA CLIFT

OUR FINAL DINNER WAS AS WE STARTED. BOEUF BOURGUIGNON. WE SPENT SEVERAL HOURS SIGNING EACH OTHER'S SKETCHBOOKS. I SO WISH WE HAD DONE THIS AFTER THE FIRST GROUP. MICHELLE AND I HAD AN INTERESTING DISCUSSION ABOUT THE SPIRITS IN THE HOUSE. AS I MENTIONED FROM THE GHOST HUNT WHEN WE ORIGINALY ARRIVED. THERE WAS A FEELING THAT THEY ARE HAPPY ABOUT HOW THE CHATEAU IS BEING USED. I AM SURE EVERYONE BRINGS POSITIVE ENERGY.

SOMEONE IN THE GROUP FOUND A STASH OF SNUGGIES AND THEY DASHED AROUND THE GROUNDS IN THEM TAKING PICTURES. THE BEST WAS A RECREATION OF AN IMAGE THE PHOTOGRAPHER WHO VISITS THE CHATEAU WITH THE MODEL FOR THE LIFE DRAWING AFTERNOON TOOK OF SEVERAL LADIES. IT IS A SIRENESQUE TABLEAU WITH

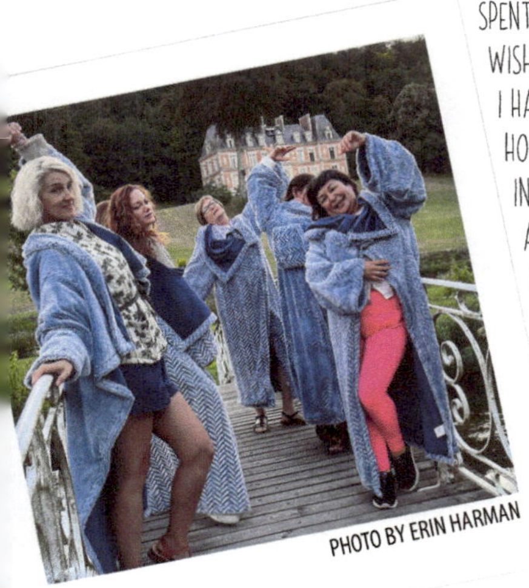

PHOTO BY ERIN HARMAN

The Snuggie sirens.

MALES CONSPICUOUSLY ABSENT THAT IS DISPLAYED IN THE BATHROOM.

I WISH I COULD HAVE STAYED UP LATER BUT WANTED TO REST UP FOR THE THREE-HOUR DRIVE TO THE AIRPORT.

DAY 28

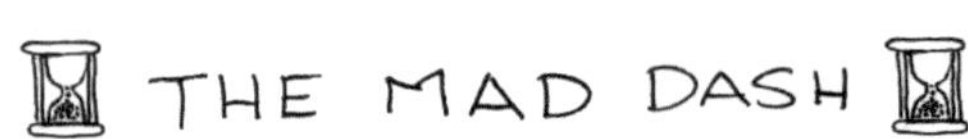 THE MAD DASH

I GOT UP SUPER EARLY TO FINISH PACKING. I HAD TO DROP THE CAR OFF AT CHARLES DE GAULLE AIRPORT AT NOON AND THEN FLY TO NICE. AFTER THE EASYJET DEBACLE, I BOOKED WITH AIRFRANCE. I COULD NOT IMAGINE THE STRESS OF TRYING TO GET TO THE ROISSY-EN-FRANCE AIRPORT.

SIMPLE IS ALWAYS BETTER IS THE LESSON I LEARNED FROM MY POST COVID TRAVEL.

I THEN WENT AROUND THE HOUSE TAKING PICTURES. THERE WAS SO MUCH I DID NOT DO AND SKETCH! HOW DID THE TIME GO SO FAST? WHY DIDN'T I TAKE THE TIME TO PAINT THE BOAT HOUSE AND THE CHURCH?

I WOULD HAVE TO PONDER THESE QUESTIONS LATER. I HAD TO SIGN THE GIANT BOOK EVERYONE SIGNS ON DISPLAY IN THE MAIN ENTRYWAY BEFORE I LEFT. I DID A LITTLE SKETCH OF DUSTY WITH MY NOTE OF GRATITUDE AND THEN PREPARED TO SAY GOODBYE. I ALSO LEFT THE PAINTINGS I DID FOR ERIC, ZIGGY, AND BEULAH IN THE DINING ROOM ON THE MANTELPIECE.

AS I WAS ABOUT TO LEAVE, I GOT A TEXT FROM ZIGGY SAYING THAT THERE WAS NOT ENOUGH ROOM IN THE VAN DUE TO A MISCOMMUNICATION AND ASKING IF I COULD TAKE RACHEL AND LAURA TO THE TRAIN STATION. SINCE IT WAS ON THE WAY TO THE AIRPORT, IT WAS NO PROBLEM. IT ALSO WAS COMPANY TO KEEP ME AWAKE DURING THE LONG DRIVE. I NEVER HAD FIGURED OUT WHERE JOJO'S HOUSE WAS IN THE VILLAGE AND I FINALLY GOT TO SEE IT.

WE SAID SOME HASTY GOODBYES AT THE STATION AND I HEADED OFF TO MY NEXT ADVENTURE LEAVING THE CHATEAU BEHIND.

THE DRIVE TO PARIS WAS UNEVENTFUL BUT I HAD TO FIND A GAS STATION TO FILL UP ONE LAST TIME. YOU SEE THEM EVERYWHERE UNTIL YOU NEED THEM AND THE COMPLETELY CONTACTLESS EMPTY GAS STATIONS ALWAYS FREAKED ME OUT A LITTLE AND THE NEXT STATION YOU SEE, THE GAS IS ALWAYS 20 CENTS LESS A LITRE. IT IS A UNIVERSAL RULE OF TRAVEL.

NEXT WAS THE CHARLES DE GAULLE AIRPORT RENTAL CAR SCAVENGER HUNT. SURE, THERE WAS A MAP ON THE PAPERWORK, BUT TRY LOOKING AT THAT WHILE TRYING TO FIND THE RIGHT PLACE TO TAKE THE CAR TO.

THE AIRPORT HAS DEPARTURE BAYS THAT ALL HAVE GATES AND CHARGE IF YOU ARE AT THEM TOO LONG. GOOGLE MAPS SENT ME TO ONE. AS I LEFT IT, I SAW ANOTHER SIGN FOR RENTAL RETURN. I HAD TO TAKE A SHARP LEFT TURN INTO A NARROW ENTRANCE INTO THE PARKING GARAGE THAT SPIRALED UPWARD. I HAD TO TAKE ANOTHER TICKET AND DRIVE FURTHER IN. I PRAYED TO EVERY RELEVANT DEITY THAT I WAS IN THE RIGHT PLACE BECAUSE I HAD NO IDEA HOW TO GET OUT OF THIS PLACE.

I ALMOST CRIED WHEN I SAW THAT ALAMO SIGN. WHEN I SIGNED THE PAPERWORK. THE WOMAN CHECKING ME IN SAID SHE HAD NEVER SEEN THE CAR RENTED FOR THAT LITTLE. I TOLD HER IT WAS THROUGH COSTCO WHICH SHE HAD NEVER HEARD OF BUT THAT IS A DEFINITE PLUG FOR THEM!

Coda

☀ *Two Days in Nice* ☀

I PLANNED TO SPEND A FEW EXTRA DAYS IN EUROPE BEFORE I WENT HOME. I CONSIDERED FLYING TO BUCHAREST TO MEET MY FRIEND IOANA WHO WAS PUTTING THE FINISHING TOUCHES ON OUR 2024 SKETCHING TRIP TO ROMANIA BUT IN THE END, DECIDED TO STAY IN NICE. IT WAS SO BEAUTIFUL WHEN I FLEW IN, THAT I WANTED TO SEE MORE.

AFTER THE HARROWING RENTAL CAR RETURN. THAT EVENING, I WAS DINING ON THE BEACH!

THE PUBLIC TRANSPORTATION WAS VERY REASONABLE AND I GOT A DAY PASS. I HAD BOOKED A RIVIERA CRUISE THAT MORNING. THEY POINTED OUT WHERE ALL THE FAMOUS PEOPLE LIVED.

I THEN EXPLORED, ATE MUSSELS, AND SKETCHED. IT WAS A PERFECT LAST DAY IN FRANCE.

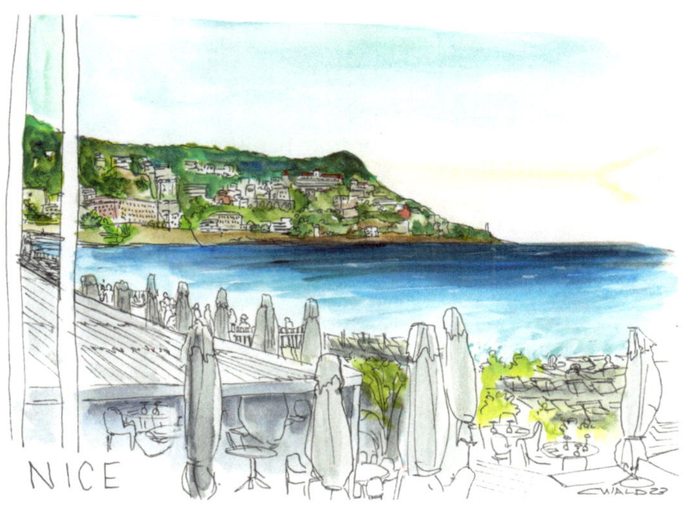

Afterward

THE BIGGEST TREAT FROM DOING THIS TRAVELOGUE WAS SAVORING ALL THE MEMORIES AS I COMPILED AND EDITED IT. I WAS SEMI-SUCCESSFUL IN INTEGRATING WRITING INTO MY SKETCHING PRACTICE AND I NEED TO DO SO MUCH MORE. NEXT TIME I WILL TRY FOR SURE.

I AM STILL DIGESTING MY EXPERIENCE AND I SUSPECT I WILL FOR A LONG TIME. IT IS A SPARK FOR FUTURE TRAVEL-OGUES AND ADVENTURES. AS ZIGGY SAYS. "EVERYTHING BEGINS WITH AN IDEA!"

– CHRISTINA WALD
CINCINNATI. OHIO
NOVEMBER 2023

ISBN-13: 9798989684106